POWER OF FEDERAL JUDICIARY
OVER LEGISLATION

ITS ORIGIN ; THE POWER TO SET ASIDE LAWS ;
BOUNDARIES OF THE POWER ;
JUDICIAL INDEPENDENCE ;
EXISTING EVILS AND
REMEDIES

BY

J. HAMPDEN DOUGHERTY

AUTHOR OF "THE ELECTORAL SYSTEM OF THE UNITED STATES"

THE LAWBOOK EXCHANGE, LTD.
Clark, New Jersey

ISBN 9781584773634 (hardcover)
ISBN 9781616190811 (paperback)

Lawbook Exchange edition 2010

The quality of this reprint is equivalent to the quality of the original work.

THE LAWBOOK EXCHANGE, LTD.
33 Terminal Avenue
Clark, New Jersey 07066-1321

*Please see our website for a selection of our other publications
and fine facsimile reprints of classic works of legal history:*
www.lawbookexchange.com

Library of Congress Cataloging-in-Publication Data

Dougherty, J. Hampden (John Hampden), 1849-1918.
    Power of federal judiciary over legislation: its origin, the power
to set aside laws, boundaries of the power, judicial independence,
existing evils and remedies / by J. Hampden Dougherty.
        p. cm.
    Originally published: New York : G.P. Putnam's sons, 1912.
    Includes bibliographical references and index.
    ISBN 1-58477-363-4 (cloth: alk paper)
    1. Judicial review—United States. 2. Judicial power—United
States. 3. Separation of
    powers—United States. I. Title.

KF4575.D62003
347.73 '12—dc21   2003052769

Printed in the United States of America on acid-free paper

POWER OF FEDERAL JUDICIARY
OVER LEGISLATION

ITS ORIGIN ; THE POWER TO SET ASIDE LAWS ;
BOUNDARIES OF THE POWER ;
JUDICIAL INDEPENDENCE ;
EXISTING EVILS AND
REMEDIES

BY

J. HAMPDEN DOUGHERTY

AUTHOR OF "THE ELECTORAL SYSTEM OF THE UNITED STATES"

———

G. P. PUTNAM'S SONS
NEW YORK AND LONDON
The Knickerbocker Press
1912

The Knickerbocker Press, New York

CONTENTS

Contents

Contents

Contents

PAGE

4Method taken by the Convention of 1787 to secure

POWER OF FEDERAL JUDICIARY OVER
LEGISLATION

POWER OF FEDERAL JUDICIARY OVER LEGISLATION

INTRODUCTION

"In truth there is at this time more hostility to the federal judiciary, than to any other organ of the government."

(JEFFERSON TO JUDGE WILLIAM JOHNSON, March 4, 1823.)

CURRENT discussion of judicial recall and recall of judicial decisions marks the recrudescence of an old heresy. Angered by the unflinching determination of Marshall and his associates on the bench to hold void not only acts of Congress but also State enactments at war with the Constitution, Jefferson asserted the judiciary to be despotic and labored for years to undermine it. "The constitution," he wrote to Judge Spencer Roane, "on this hypothesis is a mere thing of wax which they may twist and shape into any form they please." At Jefferson's instigation Roane, in 1821, published stinging criticisms of the Court in the *Richmond Enquirer* under the name "Algernon Sidney."

Resentment against judicial power had previously

taken shape in the Virginia Resolutions and the Kentucky Resolutions. It led John Randolph to introduce in Congress in March, 1805, a resolution for a constitutional amendment making Federal judges removable by the President upon the "joint address of both houses of Congress."[1] The resolution was defeated, but was renewed, in substantially the same form, in 1806, 1807, 1811, and 1816, with the added proposition that judges should hold for a term of years, not for life. In 1822 Richard M. Johnson of Kentucky offered in the Senate a resolution for an amendment to the Constitution, which is as follows:

That in all controversies where the judicial power of the United States shall be so construed as to extend to any case in law or equity, arising under the constitution, the laws of the United States, or treaties made or which shall be made under their authority and to which a state shall be a party, and in all controversies in which a state may desire to become a party, in consequence of having the constitution or laws of such state questioned, the senate of the United States shall have appellate jurisdiction.

Johnson's resolution having failed, resolutions were from time to time thereafter offered in the House for an amendment limiting the terms of Federal judges.

In January, 1838, the *Democratic Review* thus summed up the conduct of the Court under Marshall's leadership:

Nearly every state of the Union, in turn, has been brought

[1] *History of U. S.*, by Henry Adams, iv., 205.

up for sentence; Georgia, New Jersey, Virginia, New Hampshire, Vermont, Louisiana, Missouri, Kentucky, Ohio, Pennsylvania, Maryland, New York, Massachusetts, South Carolina (Delaware just escaped over Black-bird creek), all passed through the Caudine forks of a subjugation which has more than revived the suability of states. Beginning with Madison's case, there are nearly forty of these political fulminations from 1803 to 1834, viz., one each in 1806, 1812, and 1813, two in 1815, one in 1816, four in 1819, three in 1820, two in 1821, two in 1823, two in 1824, one in 1825, four in 1827, five in 1829, three in 1830, two in 1832, two in 1833, and one in 1834; a great fabric of judicial architecture as stupendous as the pyramids and as inexplicable.[1]

When the Supreme Court underwent a change of complexion shortly after Marshall's death, these efforts to curb the judiciary came to an end. Yet never was the judiciary more bitterly arraigned than by Senator Sumner of Massachusetts in his address at Faneuil Hall, when the Supreme Court upheld the constitutionality of the Fugitive Slave Law. Those distant controversies awaken only languid interest to-day. The Court's decisions were, with few exceptions, salutary and right. They made the Constitution a thing of permanence.

If to-day there is scathing criticism of the courts, the reasons are, not political, but economic. The judges, it is said, frustrate the effort of legislatures to improve social and economic conditions. In earlier days they set aside legislation only when it was "plainly and palpably unconstitutional"; now, it is said, they

[1] "Judiciary in U. S. History," Lalor's *Cyclopædia*, ii., 652, 653.

constantly substitute judicial opinion for legislative opinion as to the expediency of laws.

From the charge that the judiciary has exceeded its power, the step is easy to the charge that in setting aside laws it is guilty of usurpation. The conduct of the courts has led to an examination of the grounds of their authority to override the legislature; and we are now told that the power was never granted, that it is the result of a series of encroachments, that it disturbs the equilibrium of the three great branches of government, that nothing in the history of the States or the nation can be found to justify it, and that the judicial structure has been built upon a fallacy. This raises a question that can hardly be transcended in importance. If, for sociological reasons, restrictions are to be put upon the judiciary, no sound constructive legislation can be had, except upon the solid and enduring basis of truth.

Is it true, as is so often said to-day, that the Constitution of the United States does not confer upon the Supreme Court the power of annulling statutes, that there is not a line in that instrument to authorize it, either expressly or by implication?[1] Is it true that there is no evidence of any such purpose on the part of the Convention which framed the Constitution, that such judicial usurpation as the setting aside of a State law was a thing almost unknown when the Convention met, that it was at war with all British precedent, and

[1] According to Senator Owen of Oklahoma, "No one pretends that the jurisdiction is expressly given by the Constitution, and John Marshall ought to have known that it was expressly refused." (*Congressional Record*, August 4, 1911, p. 3696.)

that if in two or three instances State courts had exercised such arbitrary power, there is not the slightest evidence that a majority of the members of the Federal Convention or of the State conventions that ratified the Constitution knew of or approved the doctrine? These and similar statements are made not only in Congress, in the press, and upon the platform, but also in magazines of influence and before associations of lawyers and law students. Careful and impartial study of the debates in the Philadelphia Convention, and in the various State conventions, and of the history of the times in which the Constitution had its origin, will, I think, show that these modern teachings are erroneous.

The meaning and intent of the Constitution is to be learned from that instrument; not from the opinions of its framers, or their chance utterances in debates in the Convention. This proposition has the support of great judges of the Supreme Court, including Marshall and Taney. For this reason, and not because he was unaware of the views expressed in the Convention and in the ratifying State conventions, Marshall, in Marbury v. Madison, wisely resolved to seek the will of the people, not in the sentiments elsewhere expressed by the venerated authors of the Constitution, but in the Constitution itself. This deliberate resolve of Marshall has been sophistically perverted into an argument that he feared to resort to the views of the Convention and the decisions of State judges, because he knew how meagre and unreliable were the precedents holding that the judiciary could set aside laws.

If, as was said by Chief Judge Gibson, of the Supreme Court of Pennsylvania, the Constitution is supposed to contain the whole will of the body from which it emanated, and if it is not permissible to look into the debates in the Convention in order to learn its meaning,[1] nevertheless, inasmuch as this is the very course of the modern assailants of judicial power, as they keep reiterating that the most careful study will reveal no evidence whatever of any intention on the part of the Convention to vest the Federal judiciary with authority to override Federal or State legislation at variance with the "supreme law," the interest of truth requires that this challenge be met. While it is not possible to extract from the records a categorical answer to the question: Did the authors of the Constitution or the members of the ratifying conventions or the citizens they represented say, in so many words, that they meant to give the Federal judiciary the right to set aside unconstitutional laws? a great volume of material indicative of this purpose exists. The thesis here to be supported is, therefore, that the conventions and the people did intend to give the courts this power. In the progress of a century the power may have been abused. That, however, is beside the argument, which is, that the power was *intentionally and expressly conferred.*

To the main discussion which follows have been added some observations upon the necessity for an independent judiciary. Judicial recall is so direct a blow at judicial independence that it can be no cure

[1] Eakin *v.* Raub, 12 *Sergeant and Rawle*, 330, 343.

for any evils in the judicial system. There is no desire to blink the necessity for improvement, but no reform can be effected by abandoning the fundamental principles upon which the social edifice rests. Reform is not possible unless these are maintained.

THE FEDERAL JUDICIAL POWER

After the decision of the Supreme Court of the United States in Juilliard v. Greenman,[1] the latest of the Legal Tender Cases, the historian George Bancroft wrote a criticism of it entitled, "A Plea for the Constitution of the United States of America, Wounded in the House of its Guardians." To this a reply was published by Mr. Richard C. McMurtrie of the Philadelphia bar, "Observations on Mr. George Bancroft's Plea for the Constitution." In that case the Supreme Court held that, as incident to the power of borrowing money and issuing bills or notes of the government for money borrowed, Congress could make these notes legal tender for the payment of private debts. This was a power universally understood to belong to sovereignty in Europe and America when the Constitution of the United States was adopted; and as, according to the Court, there is no limitation in the Constitution upon the power of the United States in this particular, its powers in this field were held to be as plenary as those of any other sovereignty.

The argument in the Legal Tender Cases had involved the question of the jurisdiction of the Supreme Court

[1] 110 U. S., 421.

over acts of Congress and the power of the Court to declare a legislative act void. Mr. McMurtrie in his essay asked whence such a power was derived. Was such a political power ever heard of before? "Did any state before ever grant to its judicial functionaries the power of declaring and enforcing the limits of its own sovereignty? What state before conferred on a court of justice, in determining the rights of two suitors, as a mere incident, and without a hearing on behalf of the state, the power to determine that its legislative acts, approved and sanctioned by all its statesmen for thirty years, had always been mere nullities—nullities *ab initio?*" Is there, he asked, any such grant in the Constitution, or any allusion to it? Judge Marshall's opinion in Marbury *v.* Madison he declared to be a mere deduction of logic. McMurtrie's conclusion is as follows:

(1) That the power of declaring legislation to be unconstitutional and void has been created and lodged by inference, and by inference only, in one branch of the government, viz., the judicial:

(2) That there is no reference whatsoever to any such power in the text of the constitution:

(3) That no such exercise of judicial power has ever been heard of before in other civilized countries.[1]

McMurtrie's high reputation at the bar and the cogency of his reasoning were such as to require some rejoinder. Accordingly, Mr. Brinton Coxe of the

[1] Coxe, *Judicial Power*, 34.

Philadelphia bar prepared an essay on *Judicial Power and Unconstitutional Legislation*. It was published posthumously, in 1893. It has been truthfully described as "a work of vast learning, which goes over the whole general subject of the judicial power, from the broadest field of jurisprudence."[1] Its central theme is that this judicial power does not rest upon inference, but upon the express text of the Constitution, and that a similar power had been long recognized in jurisprudence. The framers of the Constitution were well aware of the foreign authorities which supported such a power. It was no new thing to the colonists or to the men of 1787 to think of an act of assembly as void and of no effect, because it violated some law of superior authority. The author's mode of reasoning was not to build upon Marbury *v.* Madison: on the contrary, he sought to show that McMurtrie was correct in the assumption that Judge Marshall's argument, if accepted, would show the power to be purely inferential and this it was the aim of Coxe to refute. Marshall's opinion in Marbury *v.* Madison moves with a majestic step and the precision of scientific logic. But a converse line of reasoning was possible, as Marshall himself knew, and it is this line that Coxe pursued. Judicial competency was matter of express import according to the constitutional text, and was intentionally granted by the makers of the Constitution, who were familiar with the history of this power. Although Sir William Blackstone in his celebrated

[1] See admirable article, "American Doctrine of Judicial Power," by William M. Meigs of Philadelphia, 40 *American Law Review*, 641, 650.

Commentaries had declared Parliament to be practically omnipotent, and Bluntschli, the great German publicist, had asserted that in most modern states there is no legal remedy against the validity and applicability of a law on the ground that its contents contravene the constitution, Coxe, in an analysis of earlier authorities, arrayed the strongest sort of proof from history that tribunals of justice have from the days of republican Rome possessed the power of arresting or nullifying unconstitutional legislation, whether the constitution was written or unwritten.

As a result of his analysis and review of foreign laws, including the Roman law and the canon law, Coxe declared that when the American colonists invented written constitutions "they did not create an unprecedented novelty in framing them upon the principle that judiciaries might decide questioned legislation to be contrariant to a constitutional or other rule of right and hold it therefore void," for there were then important precedents in Europe for such an institution. Legal history makes it clear that long before American independence there were in Europe unwritten systems of public law, according to which legislation might sometimes be decided to be contrariant to a binding right of superior strength to the legislative power exercised.[1] English law before the Revolution of 1688, the English law of the prerogative, the older French law, the older German law, the Roman law, and the canon law, he maintained, support this proposition. Investigation of the Roman law of legislative

---

[1] Coxe, *Judicial Power*, 45.

rescripts in the time of the Emperor Justinian shows that judges were given power to determine whether a rescript accorded with the general law and to reject it if they considered it contrary thereto.

Inasmuch as in certain countries the judiciary is competent to decide whether a law is unconstitutional and therefore void, and in other countries is powerless so to do, the framers of the Constitution of the United States, in approaching the subject of judicial power, were at liberty to act as they deemed wisest in bestowing or withholding this judicial competency. The Convention of 1787 was not taking a leap in the dark, for neither course was without precedents. The American precedents, such as they were, had clearly held it the duty of the courts to refuse to carry unconstitutional laws into effect.

SOME FOREIGN INSTANCES OF DECISIONS HOLDING LEGISLATIVE ACTS VOID

After an analysis of the regency cases in the reigns of Louis XIII., Louis XIV., and Louis XV., in which the Parliaments of Paris declared legislative acts of the kings of France to be null and void, Coxe says:

These French cases suffice to show that the idea of a judicial court holding legislation to be void because contrary to binding right was known in France before the time when the Constitution of the United States was framed.[1]

[1] Coxe, *Judicial Power*, 80, 81, 163, 164.

In Switzerland it would seem that the Federal Tribunal may not decide whether a federal law is constitutional or unconstitutional, nor whether the constitution of a canton contains anything at variance with the constitution of the Confederation, nor is the judiciary of a canton competent to decide whether a cantonal law is repugnant to the cantonal constitution. These questions are not justiciable for the reason probably that the Federal Assembly determines whether the constitution of a canton offends that of the Confederation. It seems also that the constitution of a canton or an amendment of it before becoming operative is subject to the criticism of the Federal Assembly.

In Germany, Mr. Coxe finds conflicting decisions. The question, however, seems to be open in that country, but he observes that the Court of the Imperial Chamber under the old German Empire did possess this authority, and he quotes from Bluntschli to prove this contention. This Court, it appears, is referred to in that celebrated number of the *Federalist*, LXXX., in which the power of the Federal judiciary over unconstitutional legislation is discussed.

Analogous powers are traced by the author in the early Roman law and, according to him, Hamilton's famous sentence, "the act of a delegated authority contrary to the tenor of the commission under which it is exercised is void," was not original with that profound thinker, but was a well-recognized principle of the Civilians, with roots extending back into early Roman jurisprudence: "*Diligenter fines mandati custodiendi sunt: nam qui excessit, aliud quid facere videtur.*"

From this source Vattel, the great Swiss publicist, who died in 1767, drew his opinions. Vattel maintained that

legislators ought to consider the fundamental laws as sacred, if the nation has not, in very express terms, given them the power to change them. For the constitution of the state ought to be fixed: and since that was first established by the nation, which afterwards trusted certain persons with the legislative power, *the fundamental laws are excepted from their commission. . . . In short, these legislators derive their power from the constitution; how then can they change it, without destroying the foundation of their authority?*[1]

In the controversies between the Church and the throne in England as far back as the time of Henry II., it seems that the same doctrine was advocated by Thomas à Becket, the famous Cardinal, in cases where the temporal statutes invaded the province of the canon law. All such legislation the canonical court held to be void "from defect of the power of the laymen enacting it."[2] In the reign of Edward II. and the pontificate of Clement V., certain statutes of the realm were held void as against the Church.

THE ENGLISH REVOLUTION OF 1688

With the Reformation, however, came a fundamental change in the English Constitution, "the partition of power between the English state and the Roman church

[1] Coxe, *Judicial Power*, 119.   [2] *Id.*, 125.

was abolished.   In ecclesiastical matters, the prerogative
of the king and the authority of parliament were no longer
restricted by anything said or done by a power seated
outside of England. . . .   Then came the revolution of
1688, giving parliament a plenitude of power in both
ecclesiastical and temporal matters, which was so absolute that no king could dispute it in the name of prerogative."[1]   It is this omnipotence of Parliament to which
Blackstone refers.

An English case which strikingly illustrates the doctrine of the right of the judiciary to annul legislation
and the danger underlying the power of judicial recall
is Geddes *v.* Hales.   It was there held that an act of
Parliament prescribing a test oath was of no validity
as against the king's dispensing power.   Macaulay de-
scribes efforts of King James II. to obtain a prosecuting
officer who would do his bidding and to fashion a court
into subserviency to his will.   This case was one of
the causes leading to the Revolution of 1688.   Having
resolved to obtain from the common law courts
an acknowledgment of his dispensing power, the
King soon found, says Macaulay, that "he had
against him almost the whole sense of Westminster
Hall."

Four of the judges gave him to understand that they
could not, on this occasion, serve his purpose; and it is
remarkable that all the four were violent Tories, and that
among them were men who had accompanied Jeffreys on
the Bloody Circuit, and who had consented to the death
of Cornish and Elizabeth Gaunt.   Jones, the chief justice

[1] Coxe, *Judicial Power*, 160, 161 *et seq.*

of the Common Pleas, a man who had never before shrunk from any drudgery, however cruel or servile, now held in the royal closet language which might have become the purest magistrates in our history. He was told that he must give up either his opinion or his place. "For my place," he answered, "I care little. I am old and worn out in the service of the crown, but I am mortified to find that your Majesty thinks me capable of giving a judgment which none but an ignorant or a dishonest man could give." "I am determined," said the King, "to have twelve judges who shall be all of my mind as to this matter." "Your Majesty," answered Jones, "may find twelve judges of your mind, but hardly twelve lawyers." He was dismissed, together with Montague, Chief Baron of the Exchequer, and two puisne (associate) judges, Neville and Charlton.[1]

The pith of the decision was that no act of Parliament could take away the king's prerogative of dispensing in his discretion with any of the laws, and that he was the sole judge of that necessity. "In this remarkable decision," says Coxe, "the Court regarded it as a judicial question whether or not a statute could bind the king in certain cases of prerogative right and regarded it as a judicial obligation to hold the statute to be invalid after answering that question in the negative. According to now prevalent American ideas, if the constitution of England had been written, and such a prerogative right had been constitutional, the Court ought to have done precisely what it did."

The cases in which before the formation of the pre-

---

[1] Macaulay's *History of England*, vol. ii., 62.

sent government of the United States, the State judiciary had condemned legislation as unconstitutional, are well known to students of early State history. It matters not that the instances in which this authority was exercised were few in number. The occasions for use of the power were doubtless rare; nor, commonly viewed, is it at all astonishing that such judicial action should have aroused opposition. The American colonists had become somewhat imbued with the later English notion—announced by Sir William Blackstone —of the supremacy of Parliament within the sphere of its operations, or translating this expression into more general terms, of the supremacy of the legislature. But whenever occasion required, they could vigorously resent parliamentary usurpation, and their courts would pronounce judgments showing the old principle still vital. If, in the first days of statehood, when the courts several times set aside unconstitutional laws there was a show of popular resentment, it arose from natural irritation that a weapon previously employed for the protection of the people against kings and Parliament was found equally effective against the people themselves in their own moments of arbitrary action. The earliest State governments were at most only thirteen years older than the national government organized in 1789, so that the cases in which judges declared laws unconstitutional would not be numerous. This essay will deal only with those whose influence was assuredly felt in the Convention of 1787. But there should precede a brief reference to the treatment of this subject in colonial times.

COLONIAL EXPERIENCE

Some of the authors who now claim the power a usurpation in America, admit that prior to 1688, English courts had declared acts of Parliament void, and that a. similar power was exercised by the judiciary in other countries. It is part of the argument of this same class of teachers to deny that previous to the Constitution the courts of any of the States of the Union exercised any such authority, and to maintain that the cases were very few, and the knowledge of them not extensive, the purpose being to inculcate the notion that when the Convention sat such a power was practically unheard of, and hence that it could not have been the intention of the Convention to confer it, the language of subdivision 1, section 2, Article III., and section 2, Article VI., of the Constitution to the contrary notwithstanding.

As to the experience of the American colonies, it should be sufficient to cite the authority of a well-known historian, whose words were written, as the lawyers say, *ante litem motam* (before this present controversy), when he could have had no motive to distort history. The historian McMaster makes these observations:

But there had developed in the course of the half century another restraint on the legislative branch of government which was not imposed by any constitution. Judges had assumed the right to set aside acts of legislation which in their opinion were unconstitutional. When and where this

2

right of the judiciary originated, what were the conditions under which it developed, who was the first man to boldly announce it from the bench, are questions which cannot be answered. But it is safe to assert that, like every other judicial idea that ever existed, it is the slow outcome of circumstances. The majority of the colonies for years before their quarrel with the mother-country had seen their laws disallowed at pleasure by the King or Queen in council. They had, therefore, become used to the idea of the existence of a body that could set aside a law enacted by a Legislature and approved by a governor. They were used to written charters and frames of government, and were accustomed to appeal to them as the source of all authority under the King. When, therefore, in their quarrel with the mother-country, it became necessary to find some reason for re-sisting the stamp-tax, the colonists appealed to a written document, and declared the tax law invalid, because it violated the provisions of Magna Charta.[1]

Specific instances are given by him and other historians. In February, 1766, says McMaster, the clerk and other officers of the Court of Hustings for Northampton County, Virginia, appeared before the bench of the Supreme Court and asked its opinion on two questions: "Was the law of Parliament imposing duties in America binding on Virginia? Would they, as officers of the law, incur any penalty by not using stamped paper?" The judges were unanimously of the opinion that the law "did not bind, affect or concern the inhabitants of Virginia, 'inasmuch as they conceived the said act to be unconstitutional.'" In

[1] *History of U. S.*, v., 394 (published in 1900).

Massachusetts, Mr. Justice William Cushing, destined to become a justice of the Supreme Court of the United States, charged a jury that certain acts of Parliament were null, and won the congratulations of John Adams for his courageous declaration.[1] Adams repeatedly asserted the same doctrine, and on one occasion in a memorable argument used these words: "The stamp act is invalid; we never consented to it. A parliament in which we are not represented had no legal authority to impose it; and, therefore, *it ought to be waived by the judges as against natural equity and the constitution.*"[2]

As early as 1761, in opposing before the Supreme Court of the colony of Massachusetts the petition of the customs officers for writs of assistance to enable them to enforce odious British tax laws, the eloquent James Otis declared: "No act of parliament can establish such a writ; even though made in the very language of the petition, it would be a nullity. An act of parliament against the constitution is void."[3]

George Mason of Virginia, author of the famous Declaration of Rights, adopted by that commonwealth in 1776, had condemned as unconstitutional a law authorizing the sale of the descendants of Indian women as slaves.[4]

In fact, as far back as 1738 and 1739, the Supreme Court of Massachusetts refused to enforce an order issued by his Majesty in Council, because the powers

[1] *History of U. S.*, v., 395, 396.
[2] Bancroft's *History of U. S.*, iii., 171.
[3] *Id.*, ii., 547.   [4] McMaster, v., 395.

of the Court, revived through the charter and the laws passed to carry the same into effect, were, in the judgment of the Court, inadequate for that purpose.

Some years ago in an article upon the origin of the supreme judicial power in the Federal Constitution,[1] Honorable Robert Ludlow Fowler, now Surrogate of the County of New York, set forth as his thesis that "the judicial power—of declaring acts of the legislature void because in conflict with the constitution of government—is very ancient in America." He also adverted to the fact that Dr. Robertson in his *History of the Reign of Charles V.*, which appeared in the year 1769, noted the similarity of the power of the justiza, the supreme judge of Aragon, to the power of the judiciary in this country. "The Aragonese," says Robertson, "had recourse to an institution peculiar to themselves, and elected a justiza or supreme judge. . . . *He was the supreme interpreter of the laws*. Not only inferior judges, but the kings themselves were bound to consult him in every doubtful case and to receive his responses with implicit deference. An appeal lay to him from the royal judges, as well as from those appointed by the barons within their respective territories."

EARLY STATE CASES

The case of Josiah Philips arose in Virginia, May, 1778. Philips was attainted by a bill of attainder passed by the Assembly of Virginia, May, 1778.

[1] *American Law Review*, Sept.–Oct., 1895.

According to this act, he was guilty of devastating and marauding within the State. He was captured in the autumn of that year, indicted, tried, and convicted of highway robbery. The act of attainder was not enforced, but it is impossible to determine whether the failure to enforce it was due to the inaction of the Attorney-General or the refusal of the Court to recognize it as valid.[1]

Commonwealth *v*. Caton, Hopkins, and Lamb was decided in the Court of Appeals, Virginia, in 1782.[2] The defendants had been condemned for treason by the General Court under an act of Assembly passed in 1776, depriving the executive of the power to grant pardon in such cases. In June, 1782, the House of Delegates passed a resolution which it sent to the Senate for concurrence, granting the prisoners a pardon. The Senate refused to concur. In October the Attorney-General moved in the General Court that execution of the judgment might be awarded. The prisoners pleaded the resolution of the lower house of the legislature as a pardon, the Attorney-General denied its sufficiency because the Senate had not concurred in it, and the General Court according to the reporter adjourned the case "for novelty and difficulty to the Court of Appeals." The judges of this tribunal were of the opinion that the treason act of 1776 did not infringe the onstitution and that pardon by resolution of the House of Delegates was invalid. In this case no law was decided unconstitutional. A resolution of one house was treated as a nullity because of the non-

---

[1] Coxe, *Judicial Power*, 220.   [2] 4 Call's *Reports*, 5.

concurrence of the other in it.   Whether the declaration was *obiter* or not, the Court unequivocally asserted its right to hold "any resolution or act of the legislature or of either branch of it to be unconstitutional and void."[1]

Rutgers *v.* Waddington was decided in the Mayor's Court of the City of New York, August 27, 1784.[2] It was the first case in which a conflict arose between an

[1] Wythe, J., who was positive in his convictions, said: "If the whole legislature, an event to be deprecated, should attempt to overleap the bounds prescribed to them by the people, I, in administering the public justice of the country, will meet the united powers at my seat, in this tribunal; and, pointing to the Constitution, will say to them, here is the limit of your authority, and hither shall you go, but no further."

Pendleton was less confident: "How far this court, in whom the judiciary powers may in some sort be said to be concentrated, shall have power to declare the nullity of a law passed in its forms by the legislative power, without exercising the power of that branch, contrary to the plain terms of that constitution, is indeed a deep, important, and I will add, a tremendous question, the decision of which might involve consequences to which gentlemen may not have extended their ideas."

But "Chancellor Blair and the rest of the judges were of opinion, that the court had power to declare any resolution or Act of the Legislature, or of either branch of it, to be unconstitutional and void; and that the resolution of the House of Delegates, in this case, was inoperative, as the Senate had not concurred in it."

[2] The account of this case in Coxe's work is drawn principally from a contemporary report entitled "Arguments and Judgments of the Mayor's Court of the City of New York in a Cause between Elizabeth Rutgers and Joshua Waddington, New York, printed by Samuel Leudon, 1784." There is a full and interesting narrative, largely compiled from the same source, by the late Honorable Charles P. Daly in a history of the Court of Common Pleas, New York County, that forms an introduction to volume i., *E. D. Smith's Reports*. The case is the subject of brief comment in McMaster's *History of the United States* (vol. i., 219, 220).

act of a State legislature and a treaty of the United States, the treaty in question being that between Great Britain and the Confederation of the United States at the close of the Revolutionary War. The decision had marked consequences, not commonly noted: it led to the resolution of the Congress of the Confederation, March 21, 1787, that was transmitted to the States in April. That resolution will be set forth later. It had important consequences in the Convention of 1787; it led to that clause of the Federal Constitution declaring the Constitution, the laws of the United States made in pursuance thereof, and all treaties made under the authority of the United States, the supreme law of the land. The case therefore merits consideration.

According to Judge Daly, the case "first drew Hamilton's attention to the consideration of principles growing out of the union of the states and the establishment of independence, principles which he afterwards elaborated in the discussion of the national Convention of 1787, in the papers of the *Federalist*, and in the debates of the New York Convention of 1788; and which were subsequently embodied in the Constitution of the United States."

In 1783, the year of the treaty, the New York Legislature enacted a law that any one who by reason of the invasion had left his place of abode might bring an action of trespass and recover damages against any person who had occupied his premises or received his goods or effects while the property was under the control of the enemy, and the statute forbade the defendant to plead or offer in evidence as a defence that the property was occupied, injured, or destroyed by a military order or command. Under this statute Elizabeth Rutgers brought action against the defendant Waddington for rent of a brew-house or malt-house in the city of New York, possession of which he had received during British occupancy of the city. Waddington pleaded possession of the city by the British army and a license from the commissary-general in 1778 to him, a British subject, to use the premises from September 28, 1778, to April 30, 1780. He also pleaded in bar the treaty of peace, by the terms of which all claims of British subjects or American citizens to retribution or indemnity for acts done during the war were relinquished and released. From the importance of the principle involved and the large number of cases depending upon its determination, covering claims to an enormous amount, it excited a degree of interest, says Judge Daly, that no single case in the State had theretofore aroused. The counsel retained in the cause included some of the most notable lawyers in the city but the leading points were discussed by the Attorney-General, Egbert Benson, for the plaintiff, and by Hamilton, in opposition, for the defendant. The Attorney-General relied upon the statute; the State, he said, had the power to enact it; Hamilton, in answer, asserted that the statute was in violation of the law of nations, which, as part of the common law, had by the State constitution become the law of the State; that the defendant was protected by the treaty of peace; that the Congress of the United States was a party to that treaty, and that it could

not violate the terms of the treaty, nor could any
State do so.

The principal features of the decision of Duane, the
Justice who presided at the trial, are thus set forth
by Judge Daly:

The defendant was liable for the rent of the premises for
the first three years, as its use, during that period, could not
be regarded as having any relation to the war. The license
from the commissary-general conferring upon the defendant
no right to the possession, that officer having no authority to
grant one; but for the remaining three years, during which
it was held under an order from Sir Henry Clinton, to whom,
or to whose agent, the rent had been annually paid, he held
that the defendant was not liable. By the law of nations,
restitution of the rents or issues of houses or land, collected
bona fide, under the authority of a commander in chief,
while in the possession of the city, during a state of war,
could not be enforced. The law of nations had become,
by the state constitution, the law of the state; and must be
regarded as a fundamental law, applicable to and in force
throughout the whole confederacy. By the federal compact, the states were bound together as one independent
nation. In respect to each other, and in their national
affairs, they exercised a joint sovereignty, the will of which
could only be expressed by the acts of the delegates of the
separate states in congress assembled. Abroad, the states
could only be recognized in their federal capacity; and
having combined together, and formed a nation, they must
be governed by the law of nations. No one state could
arrogate to itself the right of changing at pleasure those laws
which are received as a rule of conduct by the common
consent of the civilized world.

For a separate state to alter or abridge any one of the known laws of nations, was contrary to the nature of the confederacy, in conflict with the intention of the articles, and dangerous to the Union. The defendant was residing in the city in pursuit of his private affairs, taking no part in the acts of the military; and to hold under the statute, that he could not plead as a defence that he had paid for the use of the premises, to those who, in the plenitude of military power, were exercising dominion over the city, was such a clear violation of every principle of right, that it was not to be presumed that such was the intention of the legislature. It was not to be presumed that it was their intention, by the generality of the terms employed in the act, to repeal the law of nations, and violate the compact of the confederacy; it being a familiar rule, that where two laws were in any of their provisions repugnant to each other, the latter was not deemed to be a repeal of the first, unless the intention to do so was clear and unmistakable. Even if such was the intention in the passage of the act, the state had no power to make such a law. The power to go to war and to make peace was vested in the national congress. They had concluded peace by a solemn treaty, and peace worked an oblivion of the past. Nor was it necessary to inquire whether the particular amnesty embodied in the treaty would meet the defendant's case, for his defence rested upon a right included and protected by that general amnesty or immunity thereafter, for any act done during, or having relation to the war which, as between belligerents, is implied in every treaty of peace, whether expressed or not. The treaty bound the whole confederacy, and every state, and no member of the compact could alter, abridge, or impair it.

The Court, following Sir William Blackstone's theory of legislative omnipotence, declared the legislature supreme in matters of legislation. Inasmuch as Duane distinctly held that the legislature could not have meant to violate the law of nations, and that "whoever then is clearly exempted from the operation of this statute by the law of nations, this Court must take it for granted, could never have been intended to be comprehended within it by the Legislature," this conclusion, to the public mind, was equivalent to a decision setting aside the statute as in contravention of the treaty. Public indignation was intense. A public meeting was held and a committee appointed to draw up a letter to the taxpayers protesting against usurpation of power by the judiciary, and the New York Assembly passed the following resolution:

RESOLVED, That the judgment aforesaid is, in its tendency, subversive of all law and good order and leads directly to anarchy and confusion; because if a court instituted for the benefit and government of a corporation may take upon them to dispense with and act in direct violation of a plain and known law of the State, all other courts, either superior or inferior, may do the like; and therewith will end all our dear-bought rights and privileges, and legislatures become useless.

Despite public protests and legislative resolutions there was gradual acquiescence in the decision. Not only was it in accord with sound principle, but it was soon to be followed by two similar decisions in other States and by provisions of the Federal Constitution unquestionably conferring this power upon the Federal judiciary.

Trevett *v.* Weeden was heard and adjudicated by the Superior Court of Judicature of Rhode Island at Newport, September 25, 26, 1786. According to Judge Cooley this case has the distinction of being the first in which a law was declared unconstitutional and void. The Virginia case did not go to this extreme, and the New York case decided merely that the State Legislature could not be assumed to have intended to place the United States in the position of infringing the terms of a treaty.

Trevett *v.* Weeden is mentioned by Bancroft in his *History of the Constitution of the United States,*[1] and also by McMaster.[2] In May, 1786, the General Assembly of Rhode Island by law sanctioned the emission of certain paper money, and in June, 1786, provided for the imposition of penalties upon any person who should refuse to receive the authorized money at its face value in exchange for goods on sale. An act passed at a special session, August, 1786, declared that trial of offenders should take place "without any jury," by a majority of the judges present, according to the laws of the land, and that there should be no appeal from the judgment of the Court. The main issue in this case was whether the legislature could abolish trial by jury, which was guaranteed by the common law and the constitution of Rhode Island. The senior counsel for the defence was General James M. Varnum, member

[1] Vi., 169, 170.   [2] I., 337–339.

of the Federal Congress from Rhode Island, whose argument was subsequently published. "It is of the essence of Varnum's argument that there was a continuity in the constitution of Rhode Island from the foundation thereof in the reign of Charles II. down to the then year 1786," and although the colonial charter of Rhode Island lost all vigor at the Revolution as an act of the late sovereign, it continued in vigor as a part of the unwritten constitution of the new State. The powers of the legislature were created and limited by this charter, which had been granted by the King upon the petition of the people. The people of the new State might have annulled it and substituted in its place a written instrument. They had not done so, however, but continued it in existence.

If we have not a constitution, by what authority doth our General Assembly convene to make laws and levy taxes? . . . They make laws and levy taxes, and their constituents obey those laws and pay those taxes. Consequently they meet, deliberate, and enact, in virtue of a constitution, which, if they attempt to destroy, or in any manner infringe, they violate the trust reposed in them, *and so their acts are not to be considered as laws, or binding upon the people.*

It is interesting to note that Varnum cites the view of the publicist Vattel, that the legislature of any State under a constitution cannot alter the fundamental law without having in express terms the power to change the same as part of its commission. As Vattel had said, "legislators derive their power from the consti-

tution; how, then, can they change it, without destroying the foundation of their authority?" Varnum
then maintained that it was a judicial question whether
the legislature had violated the constitution or not.
The legislature has

the uncontrolled power of making laws not repugnant
to the constitution. The judiciary have the sole power of
judging those laws, and are bound to execute them; but
cannot admit any act of the legislative as law, which is
against the constitution.

The judgment of the Court, to quote its technical
phraseology, was that "the information was not cog-
nizable before them." The judges did not in so many
terms pronounce the statute unconstitutional, but they
plainly rejected and repealed the challenged statute.
The bar, the legislature, the public, understood that
the Court by its judgment meant that the statute was,
as the defendant's plea had asserted, "unconstitutional
and so void."

As Professor Thayer states,[1] the consequences of
the decision were immediate. The shops and stores
were generally opened, business assumed a cheerful
aspect, public confidence was restored, and industry
revived. But the legislature resented the defiance of
the courts. It passed a resolution condemning the
decision. It required the judges to come before it at
once and give their reasons for adjudging an act of the
General Assembly unconstitutional, and so void. Of

[1] *Cases on Constitutional Law*, vol. i., 75.

the five magistrates, three obeyed, the two others being unable to do so by reason of illness. These three were directed to appear at a later session, which they did. In the presence of a tribunal which threatened them with removal, the judges did not cower; they told the legislature that the statute was unconstitutional, had not the force of a law, and could not be executed, and that they were not amenable to the legislature for the reasons for their judgment. The Assembly, after discussion, voted that it was dissatisfied with the reasons given by the judges for their judgment in the case, and a motion was made and seconded for dismissing the judges from their office. This is an interesting illustration of what might be expected were the principle of judicial recall to be adopted. Fortunately for the reputation of the State, the resolution was not carried. Although the legislature permitted the judges to continue during their terms, it refused reappointment to all of the number save one, and in making new appointments was careful to see that the new incumbents made no such pretensions for the judiciary.

Shortly after this remarkable episode in Rhode Island there arose in North Carolina a case which evoked interest all over the commonwealth, echoes of which were heard at the Philadelphia Convention in 1787. This was Den d. Bayard and wife v. Singleton, decided by the Court of Conference of North Carolina in May, 1787.[1] This case arose under a written constitution. In this respect Coxe distinguishes it from the case of Trevett v. Weeden, which, rightly or wrongly, he con-

[1] 1 Martin, N. C., 42.

siders as having arisen under an unwritten constitution. The fundamental issue in Bayard *v.* Singleton, as in the Rhode Island case, was whether a legislature could abolish the common-law right of trial by jury. The leading counsel for the plaintiff was James Iredell, who afterwards became an associate justice of the Supreme Court of the United States. William R. Davie, afterwards a delegate to the Philadelphia Convention, and, later, Governor of North Carolina, was associated with Iredell. Iredell's interest in the subject-matter of the litigation antedated his connection with the cause. Convinced that the legislature had no power to impair the right of trial by jury and that the courts were clothed with full authority to declare such legislation void, he prepared a letter to the public which was printed at Newbern August 17, 1786. This, it is safe to say, is the ablest and most complete exposition of the power of the judiciary over unconstitutional legislation which had appeared in the whole literature on the subject.[1]

[1] Among other things, Iredell's letter said: "The power of the Assembly is limited and defined by the constitution. It is a creature of the constitution. . . . The people have chosen to be governed under such and such principles. They have not chosen to be governed, or promised to submit upon any other; and the Assembly have no more right to obedience on other terms, than any different power on earth has a right to govern us; for we have as much agreed to be governed by the Turkish Divan as by our own General Assembly, otherwise than on the express terms prescribed. . . . The great argument is, that though the Assembly have not a right to violate the constitution, yet if they in fact do so, the only remedy is, either by a humble petition that the law may be repealed, or a universal resistance of the people. But that in the meantime, their act, whatever it is, is to be obeyed as a law; for the judicial power is not to presume to question the power of an act of Assembly.

The decision of the Court was in full accord with Iredell's views. The judges held that by the constitution of the State "every citizen had undoubtedly a right to a decision of his property by a trial by jury. . . . That it was clear that no act they [the legislature] could pass could by any means repeal or alter the constitution." Like the New York and the Rhode Island case, this aroused much opposition. The leading champion of legislative supremacy was Richard Dobbs Spaight. He had been a member of the North Carolina convention that framed the State constitution, was afterwards Governor of the State, and at the time of the publication of his letter attacking the Court, was in actual attendance at the Federal Convention as a delegate from North Carolina.

"To these positions, not unconfidently urged, I answer:—

"1. That the remedy by petition implies a supposition, that the electors hold their rights by the favour of their representatives. The mere stating of this is surely sufficient to excite any man's indignation. What! if the Assembly say, we shall elect only once in two years, instead of electing annually, are we to petition them to repeal this law? To request that they will be graciously pleased not to be our tyrants, but to allow us the benefit of the government we ourselves have chosen, and under which they alone derive all their authority?

"But 2. The whole people may resist. A dreadful expedient indeed. We well know how difficult it is to excite the resistance of a whole people, and what a calamitous contingency, at best, this is to be reduced to. But it is a sufficient answer, that nothing can be powerful enough to effect such a purpose in a government like ours, but universal oppression. . . . How many things have been done by majorities of a large body in heat and passion, that they themselves afterwards have repented of! Besides, would the minority choose to put themselves in the power of a majority? Few men, I presume, are always in a majority.

.　.　.　.　.　.　.　.　.

He denied that the judiciary possessed any such power. It would, he said, "have been absurd and contrary to the practice of all the world, had the constitution vested such power in them." The General Assembly, he contended, represented the people of the State, and the people's will was not subject to the will of three individuals, the incumbents of the bench. Such power in the judges "would be more despotic than the Roman decemvirate and equally insufferable."[1] In reply Iredell, on August 26, 1787, addressed a letter to Spaight which was received during the course of the proceedings of the Philadelphia Convention.

IREDELL'S LETTER

Iredell reiterated his conviction, that an act of the legislature inconsistent with the constitution was

---

"These two remedies, then, being rejected, it remains to be inquired whether the judicial power hath any authority to interfere in such a case. The duty of that power, I conceive, in all cases, is to decide according to the laws of the State. It will not be denied, I suppose, that the constitution is a law of the State, as well as an act of Assembly, with this difference only, that it is the fundamental law, and unalterable by the legislature, which derives all its power from it. One act of Assembly may repeal another act of Assembly. For this reason, the latter act is to be obeyed, and not the former. An act of Assembly cannot repeal the constitution, or any part of it. For that reason, an act of Assembly, inconsistent with the constitution, is void, and cannot be obeyed, without disobeying the superior law to which we were previously and irrevocably bound. The judges, therefore, must take care, at their peril, that every act of Assembly they presume to enforce is warranted by the constitution, since if it is not, they act without lawful authority."

[1] McRee's *Iredell*, ii., 169, 170.

void, and that the judges would not carry it into effect. The constitution, he said, appears to be a fundamental law, which limits the powers of the legislature, and with which every exercise of those powers must necessarily be compared. Without an express constitution the powers of the legislature would undoubtedly have been absolute (as the Parliament in Great Britain is held to be), and any act passed not inconsistent with natural justice (for that curb is avowed by the judges even in England) would have been binding on the people. After depicting the danger in rule by an unrestrained majority, the letter continued:

The Constitution, therefore, being a fundamental law, and a law in writing of the solemn nature I have mentioned (which is the light in which it strikes me), the judicial power, in the exercise of their authority, must take notice of it as the groundwork of that as well as of all other authority; and as no article of the Constitution can be repealed by a legislature, which derives its whole power from it, it follows either that the fundamental unrepealable law must be obeyed, by the rejection of an act unwarranted by and inconsistent with it, or you must obey an act founded on an authority not given by the people, and to which, therefore, the people owe no obedience. It is not that the judges are appointed arbiters, and to determine as it were upon any application, whether the Assembly have or have not violated the Constitution; but when an act is necessarily brought in judgment before them, they must, unavoidably, determine one way or another.

Iredell conceded the possibility of abuse of this judicial power, but considered the danger not serious, and in conclusion said:

The power of the judges, take it altogether, is indeed alarming, as there is no appeal from their jurisdiction, and I don't think any country can be safe without some Court of Appeal that has no original jurisdiction at all, since men are commonly careful enough to correct the errors of others, though seldom sufficiently watchful of their own, especially if they have no check upon them.

There can be little doubt that the Court's decision, which had been made in May, the state of feeling which it had aroused in North Carolina, and Iredell's letter to Spaight, were well known to the members of the Philadelphia Convention.

IMPORTANT ACTION BY CONGRESS OF THE CONFEDERATION

Among the causes leading to the Philadelphia Convention was the disquietude of the government of the Confederation over the unwillingness of some States to abide by the stipulations imposed by the treaty of 1783. These had been resented in New York in the trespass act which was under consideration in Rutgers *v.* Waddington.

The Congress of the Confederation felt impelled in earnest terms to urge obedience to the treaty upon the States, and accordingly on March 21, 1787, it recommended the several States to enact identical laws of the following tenor:

> Whereas certain laws or statutes made and passed in some of the United States, are regarded and complained of as repugnant to the treaty of peace with Great Britain, by reason whereof not only the good faith of the United States, pledged by that treaty, has been drawn into question, but their essential interests under that treaty greatly affected, And whereas justice to Great Britain, as well as regard to the honour and interests of the United States, require that the said treaty be faithfully executed, and that all obstacles thereto, and particularly such as do or may be construed to proceed from the laws of this state, be effectually removed,
>
> Therefore, Be it enacted by . . . and it is hereby enacted by the authority of the same, that such of the acts or part of acts of the legislature of this state, as are *repugnant to the treaty of peace* between the United States and his Britannic Majesty, or any article thereof, shall be, and hereby are repealed. And further, that *the courts of law and equity* within this state be, and they hereby are *directed and required* in all causes and questions cognizable by them respectively, and arising from or touching the said treaty, to *decide and adjudge* according to the tenor, true intent, and meaning of the same, *anything in the said acts, or parts of acts, to the contrary thereof in any wise notwithstanding.*

The language of the resolution is a clear recognition of the propriety of judicial control over unconstitutional laws, almost insolent and defiant in its plainness of speech. Congress surely would not have advised the States to pass legislation directing and requiring the courts *to decide and adjudge according to the tenor,*

intent, and meaning of the treaty, unless supervision over
State legislation was commonly understood to be
properly within the judicial prerogative. The Federal
letter transmitted by Congress to the States together
with the resolution makes this even clearer (if that
were possible), for it declares that if its recommenda-
tion be followed, *"the business will be turned over to
the proper department, namely, the judicial; and the
courts of law will find no difficulty in deciding whether
any particular act or clause is or is not contrary to the
treaty."* That Congress should have proposed to the
States that they pass laws requiring their judges to
hold void all statutes repugnant to the treaty would
indeed be inexplicable, had the courts not possessed
such authority.

The contempt of the treaty manifest in some States
undoubtedly led to that clause of the Constitution, hereafter to be analyzed in detail, which provides that all
treaties made or which shall be made under the authority of the United States shall be the supreme law, and
that the judges in every State shall be bound thereby.

THE INTENT OF THE CONVENTION EVINCED IN TWO
CLAUSES OF THE CONSTITUTION

That the framers intended this power to be given
to the Federal judiciary established by the new Constitution, and to the State judiciaries affected by it, is
made clear in two provisions of the new Constitution.
The discussions in the Convention which led up to

these provisions, the gradual amendment of the form in which the dominant idea was originally embodied, prove that the Convention intended to establish a judicial power operating directly upon individuals in all the States, and that to achieve this end, it purposed to give to the Supreme Court the right of review of all State legislation inimical to the organic law of the Union which had been upheld by a State tribunal as not in conflict with that law and the further right to review judgments of State courts holding acts of Congress unconstitutional.

These important clauses of the Constitution, clauses upon which Webster in his great arguments in the Senate relied in support of the same doctrine,[1] are as follows:

This constitution and the laws of the United States which shall be made in pursuance thereof; and all treaties made or which shall be made, under the authority of the United States, shall be the supreme law of the land; and the judges in every state shall be bound thereby, anything in the constitution or laws of any state to the contrary notwithstanding.

The cognate clause which, together with that just quoted, establishes the Federal judiciary upon an impregnable basis, is section 2, Article. III.:

The judicial power shall extend to all cases in law and equity arising under this constitution, the laws of the United States, and treaties made, or which shall be made, under their authority, etc.

[1] *Infra*, pp. 89 *et seq.*

As will now be shown, these two clauses had their origin in the resolution transmitted by the Congress of the Confederation to the States in April, 1787, they developed side by side, and the language of one dovetails into that of the other.

As has been stated, the gravity of the situation which might arise from continued disregard of treaty obligations was keenly appreciated by the Congress of the Confederation. The first step was a resolution, unanimously adopted, March 21, 1787, declaring that State legislatures could not of right interpret, explain, or construe any national treaty or any part of a treaty, or restrain, limit, impede, retard, or counteract its operation, for all treaties made by the Confederation were part of the law of the land.[1] The resolution declared also that the treaty with Great Britain was obligatory on each State and that all acts of State legislatures repugnant to it ought forthwith to be repealed, and it was further resolved to address a letter to the States upon this subject. The letter, which was composed by the Secretary of Foreign Affairs and approved by Congress, besides complaining of State infractions of the treaty of 1783, urged the necessity of

[1] These infractions had taken the form of State laws confiscating the property of British subjects or loyalists, and releasing the patriots from their debts to all such persons, or from interest upon debts. As late as March, 1792, the British minister in this country (George Hammond) lodged with Jefferson, then Secretary of State, a formal complaint against these statutes as violations of the treaty. Jefferson replied to these charges in an elaborate letter, May 29, 1792. Jefferson takes up the various State enactments, and also a number of State decisions, among others, Rutgers *v.* Waddington.

faithful observance of all its provisions, asserted the supremacy of the Federal Congress in respect to all treaties, and declared every treaty constitutionally made by Congress binding upon the whole nation. The interpretation of a treaty, said the letter, belongs to Congress alone. The State legislatures, it continued, have arrogated power they do not possess in enacting laws that decide or point out the sense in which the citizens and courts of the State shall understand or interpret articles of a treaty. The letter closed with a recital of the resolution unanimously voted on March 21st, and urged repeal by the States of all laws repugnant to the treaty between the United States and his Britannic Majesty.[1]

THE CONVENTION'S *MODUS VIVENDI*

It would seem extraordinary that the Philadelphia Convention, held at a time when treaty infractions were the subject of solemn remonstrance by the Congress of the Confederation (which steadfastly maintained its supremacy in treaty matters), should have failed to consider a *modus vivendi*. From the provisions of the new Constitution, just quoted, it would be assumed, *a priori*, that the subject had been discussed in the Convention, and that a decision had been reached to vest the Federal judiciary with the power seemingly conferred upon it by these far-reaching provisions. The inference is in accord with fact. The power of the

[1] *Journals of Congress*, ed. 1801, vol. xii., 32–36; Appendix No. 7, Coxe, *Judicial Power*.

judiciary under the Federal Constitution does not, as was argued by McMurtrie, rest exclusively upon inference, but reposes also upon express authorization. The notion, however sedulously inculcated, that the Convention did not appreciate the meaning of the supreme law and judiciary articles is altogether erroneous. The statement, persistently made and reiterated in these later days, that nothing in the proceedings of the Convention indicates that the Convention meant to arm the Federal judiciary with the longest and most effective weapon of the State judiciary—the power to annul unconstitutional laws—is at variance with truth. Moreover, as was generally realized, the prime need of the time was the creation of a power able to coerce, not the States, but individuals. Furthermore, the Journal of the Convention unequivocally shows the views of delegates, and, apart from these utterances, the two plans urged upon the Convention—the Virginia plan and the New Jersey plan—both distinctly import an intention to give the Federal Congress some sort of negative upon State legislation. These projects were abandoned, and there was substituted the wiser notion of vesting in the judiciary a power to annul, not all laws, but those only that were unconstitutional.

AN ERRONEOUS VIEW

Honorable Walter Clark, Chief Justice of the Supreme Court of North Carolina, in an address to the Law Department of the University of Pennsyl-

vania, April 27, 1906, upon the subject, "Some Defects in the Constitution of the United States," made
the startling declaration that there is not a line in the
Constitution, either express or implicit, to warrant
the Supreme Court in assuming a power to annul
acts of Congress as unconstitutional. The Constitution, he said, recited carefully and fully the matters
over which the courts should have jurisdiction, and
there is "nothing indicating any power to declare an
act of Congress unconstitutional and void. Had the
Convention given such power to the courts it certainly
would not have left its exercise final and unreviewable." Such a power, he argued, exists in no other
country and never has existed. How wide these assertions are from the truth of history has in part been
shown and will be made clear. The power has existed
in other countries, was known even in the days of
Roman jurisprudence. Vattel expounded it, and,
while since the Revolution of 1688 no such judicial
power is recognized in the British system, nor does it
exist in the latest German Empire, Coxe and other
authors have fairly demonstrated its recognition in
other jurisdictions.

*To say that the Convention did not discuss the question
or that the Constitution is silent upon the subject is in
conflict with history.* It is in conflict also, as I hope
to show, with the plan finally evolved by the Convention
for the disposition of all controversies about State
legislation which might be at war with the Constitution
of the United States, or with treaties made by the
government, or acts of Congress. Had the members

of the Convention been able to shut their eyes to the
attempts in different States to emasculate the treaty
with Great Britain, they could not have been ignorant
of decisions like Trevett *v.* Weeden, or Bayard *v.* Singleton, which had convulsed the States in which these
judgments were pronounced.

In a debate upon the judiciary in the Convention
June 4th, Gerry said distinctly, "they [the judges]
will have a sufficient check against encroachments of
their own department by their exposition of the laws,
which involved a power of deciding on their constitutionality. In some states the judges had actually
set aside laws, as being against the constitution. This
was done, too, with general approbation."[1]

On July 17th, Madison thus referred to the case of
Trevett *v.* Weeden:

In Rhode Island, the judges who refused to execute an
unconstitutional law were displaced, and others substituted,
by the legislature, who would be the willing instruments of
their masters[2];

and on July 23d, the same distinguished statesman in
discussing the modes of ratification of the Constitution
said that

he considered the difference between a system founded on
the legislatures only, and one founded on the people, to be
the true difference between a league or treaty, and a constitution. . . . A law violating a treaty ratified by a pre-
existing law might be respected by the judges as a law,

[1] Farrand, *Record of the Convention,* i., 97.   [2] *Ibid.,* ii., 28.

though an unwise and perfidious one. A law violating a
constitution established by the people themselves would be
considered by the judges as null and void.[1]

On July 17th, in disapproving the proposed negative
of a Council of Revision, Morris[2] said that he was

more and more opposed to the negative. The proposal of
it would disgust all states. A law that ought to be negatived will be set aside in the judiciary department, and if
that security should fail, may be repealed by a national
law.[3]

Later in that day, Luther Martin moved a resolution
which marked the initial step in the creation of section
2, Article VI., and which was unanimously adopted.
This resolution was:

RESOLVED, That the legislative acts of the United States,
made by virtue and in pursuance of the Articles of Union,
and all treaties made and ratified under the authority of
the United States, shall be the supreme law of the respective states, as far as those acts, or treaties, shall relate
to the said states, or their citizens and inhabitants:—
and that the judiciaries of the several states shall be bound

[1] Farrand, *Record of the Convention*, ii., 93.
[2] Ex-President Roosevelt in his Life of Gouverneur Morris (p. 155),
says: "On the judiciary his views were also sound. He upheld the
power of the judges, and maintained that they should have absolute
decision as to the constitutionality of any law. By this means he hoped
to provide against the encroachments of the popular branch of the
government, the one from which danger was to be feared, as 'virtuous
citizens will often act as legislators in a way of which they would,
as private individuals, afterwards be ashamed.' "
[3] Farrand, *Record of the Convention*, ii., 28.

thereby in their decisions—anything in the respective laws of
the individual states to the contrary notwithstanding.[1]

If the judiciaries of the several States were to be
bound by such legislative acts in their decisions, notwithstanding contrary legislation of the State, the
implication plainly is that the judiciary must pronounce
the State legislation invalid.

Without further quotation of utterances of delegates
importing their express intent to clothe the judiciary
with this power, I now pass to consider the significance
of the plans of the Convention known respectively as
the Virginia and the New Jersey plans.[2]   The one had
its inception in the minds of representatives of the
larger States, the other in those of representatives from
the smaller commonwealths.   Neither of these plans

[1] Farrand, *Record of the Convention*, ii., 28, 29.

[2] The sixth resolution of the Virginia plan provided that the "national
legislature ought to be empowered to negative all laws passed by the
several states, contravening in the opinion of the national legislature,
the Articles of the Union."

The ninth resolution of the Virginia plan proposed a national judiciary
of one or more supreme tribunals and of inferior tribunals to be chosen
by the national legislature.   The supreme tribunal was to hear in the
dernier resort cases respecting "all piracies and felonies on the high
seas, captures from an enemy . . . and cases . . . which respect the
collection of the national revenue, and questions which may involve the
national peace and harmony."

In the New Jersey plan one of the resolutions was "that the Federal
government of the United States ought to consist of a supreme legislative, executive, and judiciary"; and the sixth resolution, following
closely the language of the resolution of the Congress of the Confederation of the preceding April, provided that all acts of the United States
should be the supreme law of the respective States, and controlling upon
the judiciary of the several States.

was acceptable in all respects to the Convention, and reconciliation was effected by the substitution of the Connecticut plan, which was a combination of certain elements of each, giving representation in the Senate to the States, as States, and in the lower or more popular legislative house according to population. One feature of the Randolph, or Virginia, plan proposed that the national legislature "be empowered to negative all laws passed by the legislatures of the several states contravening, in the opinion of the national legislature, the Articles of the Union."[1] By this phrase, "Articles of the Union," the future constitution was intended.

On May 31st, two days after its presentation by Randolph, the clause was approved and enlarged so as to include a negative of State laws contravening "treaties subsisting under the authority of the Union."[2]

Charles Pinckney unsuccessfully moved to empower the national legislature to negative all laws which to it "shall appear improper." The line or frontier which limited the negative was shadowy and indefinite, and this led to the offer by Paterson of New Jersey of his substitute plan. While it was not adopted, the offer led to reconsideration of the proposal to give a limited negative to the national legislature, with the result that by a vote of seven States to three the Convention decided to reject it.

The whole subject was thus reopened and a new plan proposed which grew out of Luther Martin's resolution heretofore quoted. Step by step this resolution was altered; each successive step marks with increasing

[1] Farrand, *Record of the Convention*, i. 21.　　[2] *Id.*, i., 47, 61.

emphasis the plain intent of members of the Convention until the culmination was reached in section 2, Article VI., and its twin text, section 2, Article III. The imperative need of some comprehensive check upon State action if a government were to be founded, the paramount importance of the creation of a tribunal to construe the Constitution, the laws, and the treaties made by the United States, and thus to avoid thirteen varying and divergent interpretations, was obvious, and the Convention would have failed to effect one of its prime objects had this result not been achieved. Its records show that it discarded the proposed legislative negative after due reflection and discussion, and that it substituted the broad judicial power after similar intelligent study.

EVOLUTION OF THE "SUPREME LAW" CLAUSE FROM THE MARTIN RESOLUTION

The precise language of the Martin resolution was referred to the committee of detail. In that committee it was changed to read as follows:

The acts of the legislature of the United States made in pursuance of this constitution, and all treaties made under the authority of the United States shall be the supreme law of the several states, and of their citizens and inhabitants; and the judges in the several states shall be bound thereby in their decisions; anything in the constitution or laws of the several states to the contrary notwithstanding.[1]

[1] Farrand, *Record of the Convention*, ii., 169.

The report of the committee of detail was considered in the Convention on August 6th, when the foregoing paragraph was read. The report was taken up article by article. August 23d, Rutledge moved to amend the supreme law article as reported by the committee of detail so that it should read as follows:

This constitution and the laws of the United States made in pursuance thereof, and all treaties made under the authority of the United States, shall be the supreme law of the several states, and of their citizens and inhabitants; and the judges in the several states shall be bound thereby in their decisions; anything in the constitutions or laws of the several states to the contrary notwithstanding.[1]

This was agreed to unanimously.

August 25th, Madison (Morris seconding) moved to add the words "made or which shall be" after "treaties," in order, he said,

to obviate all doubt concerning the force of treaties pre-existing, by making the words "all treaties made" to refer to them, as the words inserted would refer to future treaties.[2]

In this form the article went to the committee of style where, on September 12th, it was changed as follows: For the words "supreme law of the *several states*" were substituted the words "supreme law of the *land*," the words "and of their citizens and inhabitants" being omitted. The sentence "and the judges in the several states shall be bound thereby in

[1] Farrand, *Record of the Convention*, ii., 389.   [2] *Id.*, ii., 417.

4

their decisions" was altered to read "and the judges in
every state shall be bound thereby," the final paragraph remaining unaltered.[1]   September 14th, the
report of the committee of style, or committee on revision, was considered by the Convention.   Its report
was approved.   These changes made the language of
the clause exactly what it is in the present Constitution.[2]

EVOLUTION OF THE JUDICIAL SYSTEM

The clause making the judicial power co-extensive with the Constitution was not developed in its
present form until late in the sessions of the Convention.
At first the judicial power was to extend only to "all
cases arising under laws passed ·by the legislature of
the United States."[3]   On August 27th, Dr. Johnson of
Connecticut moved to insert the words "this constitution and the" before the word "laws," thus bringing
within the cognizance of the Federal Courts all cases
arising under the Constitution and acts of Congress.[1]
Madison doubted whether it was not going too far to
extend the jurisdiction generally to cases arising under
the Constitution and whether it ought not to be limited
to cases of a judiciary nature, for, said he, "the right
of expounding the Constitution in cases not of this
nature ought not to be given to that department."
Madison's suggestion was valid.   There are political
cases not within the cognizance of the courts.   Dr.
Johnson's motion was, however, agreed to *nem. con.*,

[1] Farrand, *Record of the Convention*, ii., 603.   [2] *Id.*, 610, 624.
[3] *Id.*, ii., 186.   [4] *Id.*, ii., 428.

"it being generally supposed that the jurisdiction given was constructively limited to cases of a judiciary nature." At Rutledge's instance, the words "passed by the legislature" were struck out, and after the words "U. S." were inserted, *nem. con.*, the words "and treaties made or which shall be made under their authority"—which, as the record said, was "conformably to a preceding amendment in another place."[1] This refers to the amendment placing these identical words in the supreme law clause.

To recapitulate—according to the leaders in the Convention the essential thing was a government with greater power than that of the existing Confederation and with final authority as to treaties. The vitally important question was how to reconcile legislation by the States and legislation by the Union where they might be antagonistic. To give a veto power to the national legislature would not answer, even were that veto to be restricted, as had been proposed by Charles Pinckney, to laws which should appear to be improper. The expedient of a Council of Revision involved an unwise commingling of judicial and legislative power, as the experience of New York State had already shown. At this stage the Martin resolution was offered and unanimously adopted. It proposed almost the identical thing that had been urged upon the States by Congress, in the preceding April. The acts of the Congress of the United States and the treaties made by it were to be recognized as the supreme law and the judges of the State courts were so to decide, whatever

[1] Farrand, *Record of the Convention*, ii., 430, 431.

State legislatures might enact to the contrary. This all-important resolution was never rescinded. Later the Convention perceived that in order to make the "supreme law" principle vital two additions were necessary: (1) The Constitution before all else must be deemed the supreme law; (2) Inasmuch as the State judiciary might fail in allegiance to that supreme law, a national judicial system was essential as the final authority upon all laws of the States and all acts of Congress.

In the supreme law and judiciary clauses the members of the Federal Convention created a perfect mechanism for the accomplishment of a particular end without friction between the States and the general government. Irritation, they were well aware, would continually be excited if a direct negative were given to Congress upon State legislation. After rejecting the direct negative and the proposal of a Council of Revision, they decided upon the plan of which the seminal idea is found in the Martin resolution. Despite all this, are we to believe that the Convention did not know what it was doing?

The purpose of this exposition has been to establish that prior to the formation of the existing Union, the State judiciary claimed and employed the power of adjudging laws repugnant to a State constitution to be null and void; that although this right of the judges was challenged in some instances, their conclusions were generally accepted; that these decisions were known to the members of the Federal Convention; that the existence of such a power was assumed in the resolution and letter submitted to the States by the Congress of the Confederation, in April; and that in establishing the Federal judiciary, the Convention aimed to create a tribunal which should enjoy the like prerogative, with the added power of setting aside acts of Congress inconsistent with the Constitution.

It has been shown also that there were cogent reasons why such a tribunal should be formed, because, apart from the necessity for some authority to veto State legislation antagonistic to Federal legislation, there existed the pressing need for the creation of some power to curb attempts of the States to overthrow the recent treaty with Great Britain, or by legislation to interpret, nullify, or restrict its terms. Madison from the beginning advocated some negative upon State legislation, if the new Union was to be anything more than a league. When that was found impracticable, both Madison and Wilson urged as a compromise that the national executive or the executive and the judiciary compose a Council of Revision, analogous to the Council of Revision in New York, which should have power to veto laws, that were not only unconstitutional but also, as Wilson said, "dangerous," "destructive," "yet not so unconstitutional as to justify the judges in refusing to give them effect."[1] The New York constitution of 1777 created such a council, composed of the governor, the chancellor, and the judges of the Supreme Court, with a suspensive veto of laws repugnant to the constitution, or inconsistent with the public good. This system had been in operation in New York

[1] Farrand, *Record of the Convention*, ii., 73.

for ten years, but was recognized as unwise. It persisted until the Convention of 1821, without a single dissent, voted its abolition. Mercer approved the proposed Council of Revision because he, in common with a large class of persons, disliked to have judges, sitting as such, declare laws void,—conclusive proof that the judiciary in fact exercised the power.

At this point, attention should be directed to the cardinal misinterpretation of Senator Owen, Judge Walter Clark, and their followers.

In the Senate August 4, 1911, Senator Owen read from Judge Clark's address the following passage:

A proposition was made in the convention—as we now know from Mr. Madison's Journal—that the judges should pass upon the constitutionality of acts of Congress.[1] This was defeated June 5, receiving the vote of only two States. It was renewed no less than three times, *i.e.*, on June 6, July 21, and finally again for the fourth time on August 15; and though it had the powerful support of Mr. Madison and Mr. James Wilson, at no time did it receive the votes of more than three States.   On this last occasion (August 15) Mr. Mercer thus summed up the thought of the convention: He disapproved of the doctrine that the judges, as

[1] This was a proposition to give the executive and the judges a qualified negative on acts of the national legislature before they took effect; not to confer upon courts power to nullify unconstitutional laws. The idea was borrowed from the New York Council of Revision.

Jefferson understood this plainly.   He wrote Mr. F. Hopkinson from Paris, March 13, 1789: "I approved the qualified negative on laws given to the executive, *which, however, I should have liked better if associated with the judiciary also, as in New York*" (*Documentary History of the Constitution*, vol. v., 159).   He wrote in the same strain to Madison, December 20, 1787.

expositors of the Constitution, should have authority to declare a law void. He thought laws ought to be well and cautiously made, and then to be incontrovertible.

Prior to the Convention, the courts of four States—New Jersey, Rhode Island, Virginia, and North Carolina—had expressed an opinion that they could hold acts of the legislature unconstitutional. *This was a new doctrine never held before (nor in any other country since) and met with strong disapproval.* In Rhode Island the movement to remove the offending judges was stopped only on a suggestion that they could be "dropped" by the legislature at the annual election, which was done. The decisions of these four State courts were recent and well known to the Convention. Mr. Madison and Mr. Wilson favored the new doctrine of the paramount judiciary, doubtless deeming it a safe check upon legislation, since it was to be operated only by lawyers. They attempted to get it into the Federal Constitution in its least objectionable shape—the judicial veto before final passage of an act, which would thus save time and besides would enable the legislature to avoid the objections raised. But even in this diluted form, and though four times presented by these two very able and influential members, this suggestion of a judicial veto at no time received the votes of more than one fourth of the States.[1]

The incorrectness of such inferences must be evident. The paramount demand was for an authority that should prevent constant friction between the States and the Union with respect to legislation and the interpretation of treaties. Plan after plan was proposed and rejected. The theory of a Council of Revision

[1] *Congressional Record*, 3704.

had few supporters. Then came Luther Martin's resolution, as the germ out of which evolved section 2,
Article VI. of the present Constitution. Nothing can
be plainer than that in accepting Martin's resolution,
which, be it observed, was unanimously accepted,—
the Journal says, "*nem. con.*,"—the Convention expressly intended that the courts of each State should be
competent to decide whether a State law contravened
the laws of the United States or treaties made by it,
and that the State tribunals should be required to hold
every such law of the State null and void. This solution
was in perfect accord with what the Congress of the
Confederation had in mind when in the previous April
it had resolved that the States could not "of right pass
any act or acts" derogatory to a treaty made by the
Confederation. But as because of local sentiment
State courts might fail to live up to their obligations,
the Martin resolution underwent change after change
until it took the noble, impressive, and adequate form
of the supreme law clause of the Constitution—the
clause that, under the guidance of minds like Marshall,
Story, and Webster, has made the government not a
league, but a *nation*. Yet according to Senator Owen
and Judge Clark, the members of the Convention,
men of the highest abilities, did all this unwittingly.
Study the process by which the edifice was built, and
the Owen-Clark theory will be rejected with scorn.
The theory is unhistorical, a figment of the imagination
of those who would strip the Federal judiciary of
expressly conferred power.

The "judicial veto," which according to Judge Clark

never received more than the votes of one fourth of
the States, was a proposed veto by the executive and
the judiciary combined and it was not a final veto but
a qualified or suspensive veto which received the votes
of not more than one fourth of the States.   The veto
would have been applicable not only to unconstitutional laws, but to laws which, if not unconstitutional,
would have been "dangerous" or "destructive" to the
public welfare.

The proposition four times defeated was not, as
Judge Clark assumes, one to give courts power to set
aside unconstitutional laws.   The thing which met
this signal disapproval was the plan to create a Council
of Revision consisting of the President and the judges,
with a qualified negative upon all bills passed by Congress.   The debates in the Convention nowhere show
that it refused to confer upon courts power to declare
legislation unconstitutional.   On the contrary, whenever
the subject of a Council of Revision was under consideration the members of the Convention recognized the existence of such a power in the State judges, and their
main reason for not creating a Council of Revision
was that the judges independently had authority to
declare unconstitutional laws void.

VIEWS OF MEMBERS OF THE CONVENTION

According to Professor Charles A. Beard of
Columbia University, of the fifty-five members of
the Convention present at some of its meetings, there
were twenty-five "whose character, ability, diligence,

and regularity of attendance separately or in combination made them the dominant element in the
Convention."[1]   Of this fraction seventeen, he says,
pronounced themselves, directly or indirectly, in favor
of judicial control.   John Blair, one of the Virginia
delegates, had been a member of the Virginia Court
of Appeals when The Commonwealth v. Caton was
decided.   No dissent of his was recorded from the
opinion of the Court that "it had power to declare any
resolution or act of the legislature, or of either branch
of it, to be unconstitutional and void"; hence it must be
assumed that he understood the meaning of the supreme
law clause, and the authority which the Constitution
would repose in the judges.   Wilson's views were
frequently expressed in the Convention; and Wilson,
with Blair, a fellow delegate, and Peters, while all
three sat on the Circuit Court for the District of
Pennsylvania, addressed to the President of the United
States, April 18, 1792, a letter protesting against
a recent act of Congress as devolving upon the Court
non-judicial functions.   The Constitution, says the
protest, is "the supreme law of the land.   This supreme
law all judicial officers of the United States are bound,
by oath or affirmation, to support."[2]   The opinion of
Rufus King, a delegate from Massachusetts, and
afterwards a senator from New York, was stated as
early as June 4th.   In opposing a Council of Revision,
he said that the "judiciary ought not to join in the
negative of a law, because the judges will have the

[1] *Political Science Quarterly*, vol. xxxviii., 4.
[2] See note 2 to Hayburn's case, 3 Dallas, 409.

expounding of those laws when they come before them; and they will no doubt stop the operation of such as shall appear repugnant to the constitution."[1]   Gerry, one of the delegates, on June 4, 1787, declared that "in some of the States the judges had actually set aside laws as being against the constitution."[2]   On July 17th, came the proposition to negative all laws passed by the several States "contravening in the opinion of the national legislature the Articles of Union, or any treaties subsisting under the authority of ye Union."[3]   Sherman declared this unnecessary for the reason that "the courts of the States would not consider as valid any law contravening the authority of the Union."[4]   Madison presented at length his reasons for considering the negative "essential to the efficacy and security of the general government"; but Morris opposed it, declaring that "a law that ought to be negatived will be set aside in the judiciary department."[5]   The proposition to negative was favored by Charles Pinckney, but it failed,[6] and immediately thereafter Luther Martin moved his resolution.[7]

Dickinson is to be numbered among those whose sentiments were so expressed as to show comprehension of the far-reaching scope of judicial power. While he thought that no such power as judicial control ought to exist, nevertheless appreciating the importance of establishing some authority to reconcile conflicting State and Federal legislation, he declared that he was "at a loss what expedient to substitute."   That he

---

[1] Farrand, *Record of the Convention*, i., 109.   [2] *Id.*, 97.
[3] *Id.*, ii., 21, 22.   [4] *Id.*, 27.   [5] *Id.*, ii., 28.   [6] *Id.*, 28.   [7] *Id.*, 28, 29.

had the power of the judiciary to declare legislation void plainly before his mind, and perhaps had read the famous historian Robertson, is shown by his next utterance, which is "The Justiciary of Aragon became by degrees the lawgiver."[1]

Despite the passage of the Martin resolution both Madison and Wilson returned to their favorite idea of establishing a revisionary power in the judiciary and the executive combined, Wilson saying "it had been said that the judges, as expositors of the laws, would have an opportunity of defending their constitutional rights. There was weight in this observation, but this power of the judges did not go far enough. Laws may be unjust, may be unwise, may be dangerous, may be destructive, and yet not be so unconstitutional as to justify the judges in refusing to give them effect."[2] But the Convention nevertheless adhered to the Martin resolution.

While the record of the Convention may contain no opinion upon this subject by Oliver Ellsworth of Connecticut or Alexander Hamilton of New York, they were leading advocates of the doctrine of judicial control, as will hereafter be shown. Luther Martin, author of the resolution, while opposing the Madison-Wilson theory of a Council of Revision on July 21st, said:

A knowledge of mankind, and of legislative affairs cannot be presumed to belong in a higher degree to the judges than to the legislature *and as to the constitutionality of laws, that*

___

[1] Farrand, *Record of the Convention*, ii., 299.   [2] *Id.*, ii., 73.

*point will come before the judges in their proper official
character. In this character they have a negative on the laws.*
Join them with the executive in the revision and they will
have a double negative. It is necessary that the supreme
judiciary should have the confidence of the people. This
will soon be lost, if they are employed in the task of remon-
strating against popular measures of the legislature.[1]

George Mason of Virginia supported the Madison-
Wilson plan of associating the judges with the executive
in revising the laws, using the following language:

Notwithstanding the precautions taken in the constitution of the Legislature, it would so much resemble that of
the individual states, that it must be expected frequently to
pass unjust and pernicious laws. This restraining power
was therefore essentially necessary. It would have the
effect not only of hindering the final passage of such laws,
but would discourage demagogues from attempting to get
them passed. It had been said (by Mr. L. Martin) that
if the Judges were joined in this check on the laws, they
would have a double negative, since in their expository
capacity of judges they would have one negative. *He
would reply that in this capacity they could impede, in one
case only, the operation of laws. They could declare an unconstitutional law void.* But with regard to every law, however
unjust, oppressive, or pernicious, which did not come plainly
under this description, they would be under the necessity
as Judges to give it a free course. He wished the further
use to be made of the Judges, of giving aid in preventing
every improper law. Their aid will be the more valuable
as they are in the habit and practice of considering laws in
their true principles, and in all their consequences.[2]

[1] Farrand, *Record of the Convention*, ii., 76.   [2] *Id.*, ii., 78.

Later, when the tenure of judges was under consideration, Dickinson proposed to add after the words "good
behavior," a provision making the judges removable
by the executive on the application of the Senate and
House of Representatives.   Gerry seconded the motion,
but Morris opposed it, as subjecting the judges to
arbitrary removal.[1]   Rutledge touched the core of the
matter when he said, "If the Supreme Court is to
judge between the United States and particular States,
this alone is an insuperable objection to the motion."
What else was implied in Rutledge's remark than that
the Supreme Court was to be authorized to nullify
acts of State legislation?[2]

LIGHT UPON INTENT FROM DEBATES IN THE RATIFYING CONVENTIONS

In the last analysis, the meaning of the Constitution
is to be ascertained from its language.   Nevertheless,
as it has been asserted that there is no reliable evidence
that "the majority of any one convention of the thirteen States conceived, as among the powers of judges,
that of refusing execution to statutes, or intended to
confer it,"[3] debates in the ratifying conventions should
be examined to see whether there is such evidence or
not.   Ratifying conventions were held in all of the
original thirteen States except Rhode Island, which had

---

[1] Farrand, *Record of the Convention*, ii., 428.   [2] *Id.*, ii., 428.

[3] "Judicial Dispensation from Congressional Statutes," by Dean
William Trickett, of the Dickinson Law School, *American Law Review*,
vol. xli., 82.

refused to send any delegates to the Philadelphia Convention. In most of these conventions the vote for ratification was, if New York be excepted, large; in some of the smaller States, it was unanimous. It must be presupposed that the members of these conventions comprehended the arguments both for and against ratification to which they listened. From these arguments it can be determined whether they had an intelligent conception of the mighty nature of the power to be lodged in the Federal judiciary. They could not of course foresee the wonderful expansion of that power, or its innumerable applications; but they did certainly perceive that it was designed to operate upon Congressional and State legislation, and that the judges were to be clothed with authority to nullify legislation that expressly contravened the new Constitution. To go farther—the people in the several States were through their conventions fully informed of the purpose of the Philadelphia Convention in framing those twin provisions of the Constitution upon which the Federal judiciary reposes.

The great arguments for ratification made in the Pennsylvania convention by James Wilson could profitably be read to-day. Wilson had been a delegate to the Convention, and was afterwards a justice of the Supreme Court of the United States. His fundamental theme was that all power emanated from the people, who had distributed it among the State governments and the government of the Union. Concerning the judicial power he said:

Under this Constitution, the legislature may be re-
strained, and kept within its prescribed bounds, by the
interposition of the judicial department.   This I hope, sir,
to explain clearly and satisfactorily.   I had occasion, on a
former day, to state that the power of the *Constitution* was
paramount to the power of the *legislature* acting under that
Constitution; *for it is possible that the legislature, when acting
in that capacity, may transgress the bounds assigned to it, and
an act may pass, in the usual mode, notwithstanding that
transgression;* but when it comes to be discussed before *the
judges,*—when they consider its principles, and find it to be
incompatible with the superior power of the Constitution,—
it is their duty to pronounce it void; and judges independent,
and not obliged to look to every session for a continuance of
their salaries, will behave with intrepidity, and refuse to the
act the sanction of judicial authority.   In the same manner,
the President of the United States could shield himself,
and refuse to carry into effect an act that violates the
Constitution.

.   .   .   .

The article respecting the judicial department is objected
to as going too far, and is supposed to carry a very indefinite
meaning.   Let us examine this: "The judicial power shall
extend to all cases, in law and equity, *arising under this
Constitution and the laws of the United States.*"   Controversies may certainly arise under this Constitution and the
laws of the United States, and is it not proper that there
should be judges to decide them?   The honorable gentleman from Cumberland (Mr. Whitehill) says that laws may
be made inconsistent with the Constitution; and that
therefore the powers given to the judges are dangerous.   For
my part, Mr. President, I think the contrary inference true.
If a law should be made inconsistent with those powers vested

by this instrument in Congress, the judges, as a consequence of their independence, and the particular powers of government being defined, will declare such law to be null and void; for the power of the Constitution predominates. Anything, therefore, that shall be enacted by Congress contrary thereto, will not have the force of law.[1]

Pennsylvania was the first State to hold a convention. It is well known that the debates in that body were read in other States. Wilson's sharply defined position upon the judicial power could not have been misunderstood.

In the Virginia ratifying convention no one spoke more elaborately nor opposed the judicial power more forcibly than did Patrick Henry. From his various utterances it is apparent that he keenly appreciated that the State judges could annul unconstitutional State legislation, and that like authority was to be given, with addition, to the new Federal judiciary. Henry said:

But what will the judges determine when the states and federal authority come to be contrasted? Will your liberty then be secure, when the congressional laws are declared paramount to the laws of your state, and the judges are sworn to support them?[2]

The honorable gentleman did our judiciary honor in saying that they had firmness to counteract the legislature in some cases. *Yes sir, our judges opposed the acts of the legislature. We have this landmark to guide us.* They had fortitude to declare that *they were the judiciary and would*

[1] Elliot's *Debates*, ii., 445–6, 489.
[2] Patrick Henry, *Life and Correspondence*, iii., 500.

5

oppose unconstitutional acts.   Are you sure that your federal
judiciary will act thus?   Is that judiciary so well constructed and so independent of the other branches as our
state judiciary?   Where are the landmarks in this government?   I will be bold to say you cannot find any in it.   *I
take it as the highest encomium on this country that the acts
of the legislature, if unconstitutional, are liable to be opposed by
the judiciary.*[1]

On June 20, 1788, while the first and second sections
of the third article were under consideration, Mr. Henry,
following Mr. Madison, said:

In what a situation will your judges be when they are
sworn to preserve the Constitution of the State, and of the
general government!   If there be a concurrent dispute
between them, which will prevail?   They cannot serve two
masters struggling for the same object.   *The laws of Congress being paramount to those of the states, and to their constitutions also, whenever they come in competition, the judges
must decide in favor of the former. . . .*
When Congress, by virtue of this sweeping clause, will
organize these courts, *they cannot depart from the Constitution; and their laws in opposition to the Constitution would be
void.*[2]

Marshall, answering Henry:

With respect to its cognizance in all cases arising under
the Constitution and the laws of the United States, he says
that, the laws of the United States being paramount to the
laws of the particular states, there is no case but what this

[1] Patrick Henry, *Life and Correspondence,* iii., 517.
[2] *Id.,* iii., 561, 563.

will extend to.   Has the government of the United States power to make laws on every subject?   Does he understand it so?   Can they make laws affecting the mode of transferring property, or contracts, or claims, between citizens of the same state?   Can they go beyond the delegated powers?   *If they were to make a law not warranted by any of the powers enumerated, it would be considered by the judges as an infringement of the Constitution which they are to guard.   They would not consider such a law as coming under their jurisdiction.* They would declare it void.[1]

Grayson, speaking upon the same theme, said:

If the Congress cannot make a law against the constitution I apprehend it cannot make a law to abridge it.   The judges are to defend it.

He truthfully exclaimed [2]:   "This court has more power than any court under heaven."

Governor Randolph, following Grayson, said:

Nothing is granted which does not belong to a federal judiciary.   Self-defence is its first object.   Has not the constitution said that the states shall not use such and such powers, and given exclusive powers to Congress?   If the state judiciaries could make decisions conformable to the laws of their states, in derogation to the general government, I humbly apprehend that the federal government would soon be encroached upon.[3]

Both friends and foes of the Constitution admitted that the judiciary enjoyed the power of nullifying

[1] Elliot's *Debates*, iii., 553.   [2] *Ibid.*, 564.   [3] *Ibid.*, 570.

unconstitutional laws. It passes belief that a doctrine
conceded in the Virginia convention and stated as
indisputable by Wilson in the Pennsylvania convention
was a novelty!

Pendleton, who had been a member of the Virginia
Court of Appeals that decided Commonwealth *v.*
Caton,[1] said:

> The very inference is that oppressive laws will not be
> warranted by the constitution, nor attempted by our repre-
> sentatives, who are selected for their ability and integrity,
> and that honest independent judges will never admit an
> oppressive construction.[2]

Luther Martin, author of the celebrated resolution,
left the Philadelphia Convention before the close of its
proceedings and opposed the Constitution in Maryland.
In an address to the legislature of that State, he criticised the third article creating the judicial power. No
member of the Maryland legislature could have been in
doubt as to the power conferred, for he said:

> Whether, therefore, any *laws* or *regulations* of the *Congress*,
> or any *acts* of its *president*, or other *officers* are *contrary to*,
> or not *warranted* by the constitution, *rests only with the
> judges*, who are *appointed by* Congress to determine, by
> whose determination *every State* must be bound.[3]

While he did not expressly attack the provisions

[1] George Wythe, who sat with Blair and Pendleton upon the bench
that decided Commonwealth *v.* Caton, was also a member of the
Virginia convention.

[2] Elliot's *Debates*, iii., 548.

[3] Farrand, *Record of the Convention*, iii., 220.

bringing State judgments under review by the Supreme Court, the tenor of his argument shows his appreciation of the existence of that power of review.

In the South Carolina convention Charles Pinckney, a delegate to the Federal Convention, thus spoke:

The judicial he conceived to be at once the most important and intricate part of the system. That a supreme federal jurisdiction was indispensable, cannot be denied. It is equally true that, in order to insure the administration of justice, it was necessary to give it all the powers, original as well as appellate, the Constitution has enumerated; without it we could not expect a due observance of treaties— that the state judiciary would confine themselves within their proper sphere, or that general sense of justice pervade the Union which this part of the Constitution is intended to introduce and protect—that much, however, would depend upon the wisdom of the legislatures who are to organize it— that, from the extensiveness of its powers, it may be easily seen that, under a wise management, this department might be made the keystone of the arch, the means of connecting and binding the whole together, of preserving uniformity in all the judicial proceedings of the Union—that, in republics, much more (in time of peace) would always depend upon the energy and integrity of the judicial than on any other part of the government—that, to insure these, extensive authorities were necessary; particularly so were they in a tribunal constituted as this is, whose duty it would be not only to decide all national questions which should arise within the Union, but to control and keep the state judicials within their proper limits whenever they shall attempt to interfere with its power.[1]

[1] Elliot's *Debates*, iv., 257, 258.

Pinckney occupied in that convention a place analogous to Wilson's in the Pennsylvania convention.

William R. Davie, who had been associated with Iredell as one of the counsel for the plaintiff in Bayard *v.* Singleton, was a member of the Convention of 1787, and afterwards a delegate in the North Carolina convention of 1788. In this last convention he declared in favor of plenary judicial power, taking the same stand as Iredell had taken in his "Letter of An Elector," his reply to Spaight, and his answer to George Mason's "Objections to the Constitution." Davie said:

I take it, therefore, that there is no rational way of enforcing the laws but by the instrumentality of the judiciary. From these premises we are left only to consider how far the jurisdiction of the judiciary ought to extend. It appears to me that the judiciary ought to be competent to the decision of any question arising out of the Constitution itself. On a review of the principles of all free governments, it seems to me only necessary that the judicial power should be co-extensive with the legislative. . . . Every member who has read the Constitution with attention must observe that there are certain fundamental principles in it, both of a positive and negative nature, which, being intended for the general advantage of the community, ought not to be violated by any future legislation of the particular states. Every member will agree that the positive regulations ought to be carried into execution, and that the negative restrictions ought not to be disregarded or violated. Without a judiciary, the injunctions of the Constitution may be disobeyed, and the positive regulations neglected or contravened. . . .

With respect to the prohibitory provision—that no duty

or impost shall be laid by any particular state—which is so highly in favor of us and the other non-importing states, the importing states might make laws laying duties notwithstanding, and the Constitution might be violated with impunity, if there were no power in the general government to correct and counteract such laws. This great object can only be safely and completely obtained by the instrumentality of the federal judiciary. Would not Virginia, who has raised many thousand pounds out of our citizens by her imports, still avail herself of the same advantage if there were no constitutional power to counteract her regulations? If cases arising under the Constitution were left to her own courts, might she not still continue the same practices? But we are now to look for justice to the controlling power of the judiciary of the United States. If the Virginians were to continue to oppress us by laying duties, we can be relieved by a recurrence to the general judiciary. This restriction in the Constitution is a fundamental principle, which is not to be violated, but which would have been a dead letter, were there no judiciary constituted to enforce obedience to it.[1]

With almost clairvoyant foresight, Davie shows the Supreme Court annulling State laws oppressive to the people of sister States.

States might pass most iniquitous installment laws procrastinating the payment of debts due from every citizen for years—nay for ages. Is it probable that we should get justice from their own judiciary, who might consider themselves obliged to obey the laws of their own state? Where then are we to look for justice? What is the judiciary of

[1] Elliot's *Debates*, iv., 156, 157.

the United States? . . . It is therefore necessary that the judiciary of the Union should have jurisdiction in all cases arising in law and equity under the Constitution.[1]

In the North Carolina convention, when the second clause of the sixth article was read, Iredell explained it.[2]

Spaight supported the Constitution in the North Carolina convention. Answering an objector to the judiciary article (Article III., sections 1 and 2) who had said:

I wish that the Federal Court should not interfere or have anything to do with controversies to the decisions of which state judiciaries might be fully competent, nor with such controversies as must carry the people a great way from home[3],

Spaight used these words:

The gentleman objects to the cognizance of all cases in

[1] Cases involving such laws were Sturges v. Crowninshield, 4 Wheat., 209; and Ogden v. Saunders, 12 Wheat., 214.

[2] The historian Bancroft recognized Iredell as "the master mind in the North Carolina convention." Before he was forty years old Washington had placed him upon the Supreme bench of the United States. He was supported in the convention by William Richardson Davie, who had gained high honor in the war and at the bar and afterwards held high places in North Carolina and in the Union; by Samuel Johnston, Archibald MacLaine, and Richard Dobbs Spaight. "Washington, it is said, derived his conviction of Iredell's merit from a perusal of the debates in the North Carolina convention " (McRee's *Iredell*, ii., 273). Iredell was appointed an Associate Justice of the Supreme Court in 1790, shortly after North Carolina entered the Union. He died in the same year as Washington, at the age of forty-eight years. (Bancroft's *History of the United States*, vi., 461; Moore's *N. C.*, i., 384.)

[3] Elliot's *Debates*, iv., 136.

law and equity arising under the constitution and the laws of the United States. This is very astonishing. When any government is established, it ought to have power to enforce its laws, or else it might as well have no power. What but that is the use of a judiciary? [1]

Spaight's protest against judicial control in his letter to Iredell has been assigned by some an importance beyond its merits. If, when he wrote it, he was convinced that the North Carolina court had been more despotic than Appius Claudius and his fellow-decemvirs, he was abnormally silent ever afterwards upon the subject of judicial despotism. His silence has been used as an argument to show that the Philadelphia Convention did not suspect it was conferring any of the "enormous power" which the judiciary now exercises. It has been said that Spaight "would have made the halls in which the Convention met ring to the echo with his emphatic protest, had he suspected any such implication." This is mere rhetoric. Spaight, I am inclined to think, was convinced of his errors by Iredell's rejoinder. He could not have failed to know the views of the most influential members of the Convention, for we have seen how openly they were expressed. He must have been defective in perception if he did not comprehend the meaning of the judiciary and the "supreme law" clauses. He sat with Davie and Iredell in the first North Carolina convention, and heard Davie's explicit declaration that the new Supreme Court could nullify both acts of State legislatures and laws of Congress at

[1] Elliot's *Debates*, iv., 139.

variance with the new Constitution. Spaight not only
signed the Constitution at Philadelphia, but voted to
ratify in the first North Carolina convention, and
when the second convention finally ratified, wrote
Iredell that he was "happy to hear that wisdom has
presided in our councils and enabled the convention to
break through that cloud of ignorance and villainy
which has so long obscured our political horizon."[1]
This letter, November 26, 1789, was penned *notwithstanding the fact that the first Congress had enacted the judiciary law of September 24, 1789*, section 25 of which
in plainest terms recognized the power of the Supreme
Court to set aside acts of State legislatures as well
as acts of Congress inimical to the Constitution.

The report of the debate in the Massachusetts convention shows that on January 28, 1788, and the two
following days, the second and third articles of the
Constitution were taken up and fully discussed.

Elbridge Gerry transmitted the proposed Constitution to the President of the Senate and the Speaker of
the House of Representatives of Massachusetts, and in
his letter of transmission, October 18, 1787, expressing
his disapproval, said:

My principal objections to the plan, are, that there is no
adequate provision for a representation of the people—that
they have no security for the right of election—that some
of the powers of the legislature are ambiguous, and others
indefinite and dangerous—that the executive is blended
with, and will have an undue influence over, the legislature—

[1] McRee's *Life of Iredell*, ii., 264, 273.

that the judicial department will be oppressive—that treaties of the highest importance may be formed by the president with the advice of two thirds of a quorum of the senate—and that the system is without the security of a bill of rights.[1]

What else could he have meant by the expression, "the judicial department will be oppressive," than that its power to nullify legislation might prove tyrannical?[2]

In the Connecticut convention, Oliver Ellsworth made a thorough explanation of the proposed judiciary system, and asserted that a coercive principle was necessary for the Union. It should be, however, a coercion of law, not of arms. The judicial department was designed to furnish the constitutional check both upon Congress and State legislatures.

If the United States go beyond their powers, if they make a law which the constitution does not authorize, it is void; and the judicial power, the national judges, who, to secure their impartiality, are to be made independent, will declare it to be void. On the other hand, if the states go beyond their limits, if they make a law which is a usurpation upon the federal government, the law is void; and upright, independent judges will declare it to be so.[3]

[1] Farrand, *Record of the Convention*, iii., 128.

[2] A document in Gerry's handwriting was found among the King MSS., headed "Mr. Gerry's Objections." One reads: "The Judiciary will be a Star Chamber" (Farrand, *Record of the Convention*, ii., 635).

[3] Elliot's *Debates*, ii., 196; Farrand, iii., 240.

To Ellsworth's remarks in the Connecticut convention I shall recur later in presenting Mr. Webster's views.

Ellsworth was the author of "Letters of a Landholder" which were published in the *Connecticut Courant*, Hartford, and in the *American*

Three papers by Hamilton in the *Federalist*[1] also
tend to refute the notion that the Philadelphia Convention did not mean to establish a national judiciary with
a negative upon State and Congressional legislation at
variance with the supreme law of the land.   These

Mercury, Litchfield, Connecticut. These Letters "had a wide circu-
lation, numbers being reprinted as far north as New Hampshire and as
far south as Maryland. They called out several replies" (Ford's
Essays on the Constitution, 137).

In a letter written by the "Landholder" to Luther Martin, Ellsworth credits Martin with originating the supreme law clause of the
Constitution.

In one of his replies to the "Landholder," Martin expressly admits that
he originated the supreme law clause and that he voted for an appeal to
the supreme judiciary of the United States for the correction of all
errors both in law and in fact. He rests his objection to article III,
as finally formed on the ground that it gave the judges the dangerous
and alarming power of setting at naught a verdict of the jury, thus
leaving the determination of the facts to the judges themselves.

Martin, in his letter to the citizens of Maryland, March 25, 1788,
opposing the Constitution, neither denies his responsibility for that
clause nor criticises the grant of judicial power over legislation. His
chief objection to the judiciary article was that it should have included
a bill of rights, and that jury trials would not be had in a great variety
of cases (Farrand, *Record of the Convention*, ii., 271, 295).

[1] "I have read every performance which has been printed on one side
and the other of the great question lately agitated (so far as I have been
able to obtain them) and, without an unmeaning compliment, I will say
that I have seen no other so well calculated (in my judgment) to produce
conviction on an unbiassed mind, as the *Production* of your *Triumvirate*
[the *Federalist*]. When the transient circumstances and fugitive
performances which attended this *Crisis* shall have disappeared, that
work will merit the Notice of Posterity; because in it are candidly
and ably discussed the principles of freedom and the topics of government, which will be always interesting to mankind so long as they shall
be connected in Civil Society." (Washington to Hamilton, August
28, 1788. Reprinted in *Doc. Hist. of the Constitution of the U. S.*, vol.
v., p. 33.)

papers were read and criticised in other States than New
York.   Hamilton, like Iredell, was a conspicuous advo-
cate of plenary judicial power.   In one of these papers
(No. LXXVIII.) he deals with the power of courts to
declare void any law at variance with the constitution of
a State; in another (No. LXXX.), with the judicial
system proposed by the Convention of 1787, and its
authority over State legislation and Congressional
enactments inimical to the new Constitution.   His
opinions were the outgrowth of his study in the case
of Rutgers *v.* Waddington.   Seizing with his usual per-
spicacity upon essential features, he urged that the
authority which could declare the acts of another void
must necessarily be superior to the one whose acts may
be declared void.

In No. LXXVIII. of the *Federalist*, Hamilton said:

Some perplexity respecting the right of the courts to
pronounce legislative acts void, because contrary to the
constitution, has arisen from an imagination that the doctrine would imply a superiority of the judiciary to the legislative power.   It is urged that the authority which can
declare the acts of another void, must necessarily be superior to the one whose acts may be declared void.   *As this
doctrine is of great importance in all the American constitutions*, a brief discussion of the grounds on which it rests
cannot be unacceptable.

There is no position which depends on clearer principles,
than that every act of a delegated authority, contrary to the
tenor of the commission under which it is exercised, is void.
No legislative act, therefore, contrary to the constitution,
can be valid.   To deny this, would be to affirm, that the

deputy is greater than his principal; that the servant is above his master; that the representatives of the people are superior to the people themselves; that men, acting by virtue of powers, may do not only what their powers do not authorize, but what they forbid.

It can be of no weight to say, that the courts, on the pretence of a repugnancy, may substitute their own pleasure to the constitutional intentions of the legislature. This might as well happen in the case of two contradictory statutes; or it might as well happen in every adjudication upon any single statute. The courts must declare the sense of the law; and if they should be disposed to exercise WILL instead of JUDGMENT, the consequence would equally be the substitution of their pleasure to that of the legislative body. The observation, if it proved anything, would prove that there ought to be no judges distinct from that body.

In No. LXXX. of the *Federalist*, in a further consideration of the powers of the judicial department, Hamilton thus argued that there ought always to be a constitutional method of giving efficacy to constitutional provisions:

The first point depends upon this obvious consideration, that there ought always to be a constitutional method of giving efficacy to constitutional provisions. What, for instance, would avail restrictions on the authority of the state legislatures, without some constitutional mode of enforcing the observance of them? The states, by the plan of the convention, are prohibited from doing a variety of things; some of which are incompatible with the interests of the union, others with the principles of good government. The imposition of duties on imported articles, and the

emission of paper money, are specimens of each kind.   No
man of sense will believe that such prohibitions would be
scrupulously regarded, without some effectual power in the
government to restrain or correct the infractions of them.
*This power must either be a direct negative on the state laws, or
an authority in the federal courts, to overrule such as might be
in manifest contravention of the articles of union.*   There is
no third course that I can imagine.   *The latter appears to
have been thought by the convention preferable to the former,
and I presume will be most agreeable to the states.*

In repelling the false notion that the power might be
in the State courts, he said:

Thirteen independent courts of final jurisdiction over the
same causes, arising upon the same laws, is a hydra in government, from which nothing but contradiction and confusion can proceed.

In No. XLIV. of the *Federalist*, Hamilton thus re-
minds his readers of the efficacy of the judicial power:

If it be asked, what is to be the consequence, in case *the
congress shall misconstrue this part of the constitution, and
exercise powers not warranted by its true meaning?* I answer,
the same as if they should misconstrue or enlarge any other
power vested in them; as if the general power had been
reduced to particulars, and any one of these were to be
violated; *the same, in short, as if the state legislatures should
violate their respective constitutional authorities.* In the
first instance, the success of the usurpation will depend on
the executive and judiciary departments, which are to
expound and give effect to the legislative acts; and in the
last resort, a remedy must be obtained from the people, who

can, by the election of more faithful representatives, annul the acts of the usurpers.

The evidence upon the subject has by no means been exhausted. Nevertheless, there has been mustered a vast array of proof that the delegates to the Convention of 1787 did not frame its judiciary articles in ignorance of their meaning, and that the delegates to the ratifying conventions were sufficiently admonished as to the ability of the new judicial power to veto unconstitutional laws, State and Federal. Doubtless they could not have foreseen the extent to which the power would expand in a century under the influence of judicial interpretation. In No. LXXX. of the *Federalist* Hamilton presumes a conscious purpose in the members of the Federal Convention to confer upon the new judiciary this power of overriding unconstitutional legislation, and implies that the State conventions, if they ratified the Constitution, would mean to approve this action of the Convention of 1787. As a delegate to Philadelphia, a member of New York's ratifying convention, a writer in the *Federalist*, and a correspondent of influential citizens in other States, Hamilton was assuredly in a position to know the views of his contemporaries upon this transcendently important subject. That the Philadelphia Convention deliberately intended to create a branch of the government which might negative State laws at variance with the fundamental law of the Union, and nullify acts of Congress at war with that organic law, and that it meant to give the courts the ultimate interpretation of treaties (save where the questions were purely political), the proofs cited seem convincing. The members of the Convention knew the situation which then encompassed the Congress of the Confederation and were aware that State legislatures were usurping power to determine the scope and meaning of the treaty with Great Britain. They knew also that the Congress of the Confederation, protesting against this usurpation, had urged the States not only to repeal all such legislation but to have their judges declare it void. They all shared the sentiment then widely prevalent that the Federal legislature would be prone to tyranny, and that some adequate check upon its otherwise irresponsible power must be found. This was the problem they sought to solve. Their solution was the device of the Federal judiciary. To argue that they did not intend this solution is to contradict their repeated utterances and to discredit their intelligence.

THE JUDICIARY ACT OF 1789

The provisions of the Constitution were not self-executing. They were supplemented by the Judiciary Act, passed September 25, 1789. In the framing of this act members of the late Federal Convention who had become members of the Senate and of the House of Representatives participated. Unless the violent assumption is to be made that this act was not at all in accordance with the purpose of the makers of the Constitution it must be treated as evincing their intent. It

6

has frequently and justly been cited as a contemporary construction of the Constitution.   Oliver Ellsworth and William Johnson of Connecticut, Robert Morris of Pennsylvania, William Paterson of New Jersey, were members of the first Senate and voted in favor of the act; in the House of Representatives which approved the measure was Abraham Baldwin of Georgia, who in a speech in that body, June 19, 1789, admitted that it was the province of the judiciary "to decide upon our laws," and that if they should find any unconstitutional, the courts would "not hesitate to declare it so."   Richard Bassett of Delaware and George Wythe of Virginia, one of the bench of the Court of Appeals which had decided the case of Commonwealth *v.* Caton, were also members of the House, and took prominent part in shaping this legislation.   All these men had been conspicuous in the Philadelphia Convention.

Nothing could be plainer than section 25, relating to that portion of the appellate jurisdiction of the Supreme Court which makes it the final judge of the constitutionality of State and Federal legislation.   Section 25 provided as follows:

A final judgment or decree in any suit, in the highest court of law or equity of a state in which a decision in the suit could be had, where is drawn in question the validity of a treaty or statute of, or an authority exercised under, the United States, and the decision is against their validity; . . . or where is drawn in question the construction of any clause of the Constitution, or of a treaty or statute of, or commission held under, the United States, and the decision is against the title, right, privilege, or exemption specially set up or claimed by either party, under such clause of the said Constitution, treaty, statute, or commission,—may be re-examined and reversed or affirmed in the Supreme Court of the United States upon a writ of error.

BIRTH OF THEORY OF LIMITED JUDICIAL POWER

History furnishes convincing proof as to the date when the doctrine that the Supreme Court has no power to set aside legislation was first explicitly announced. It never appeared until the formulation of the Virginia and Kentucky resolutions in 1798, 1799. These resolutions denied this power, and asserted the right of the separate States to judge whether acts of their own legislatures conflicted with the organic law of the Union, and to repudiate acts of Congress which they deemed unconstitutional—doctrines that would have been subversive of the Federal government, had they prevailed. The governors of Kentucky and Virginia transmitted copies of the resolutions to the governors of other States for approval. The only responses, all of which were antagonistic in character, came from Delaware, Rhode Island, Massachusetts, New Hampshire, Vermont, and New York.[1] These were all of similar purport, and declared that the judicial power of the United States was the sole and ultimate authority to decide upon the constitutionality, not only of State legislation, but of any act or law of the Congress of the United States. The Massachusetts resolutions denied the right of any

[1] Kentucky and Virginia Resolutions, Lalor, ii., 673; McMaster, ii., 495; *P. S. Q.*, xxvii., 27, note 2.

State legislature "to judge of the acts and measures of the Federal government." The New Hampshire resolutions declared that the State legislatures were not " the proper tribunals to determine the constitutionality of the laws of the general government; that the duty of decision was properly and exclusively confided to the judicial department." Vermont's resolutions were almost in the same words. It is in the Virginia and Kentucky resolutions that the first outspoken revolt against judicial control appears. At that time the notion took its rise that the courts could not annul legislation. Naturally advocates of the new theory, although they were few in number, were heard in the debate over the judiciary system which took place in Congress early in 1802 within a year after Jefferson's inauguration.

Before 1801 the Supreme Court had consisted of six justices who held two terms a year at the Federal capital; and twice a year they served in circuits, each justice sitting in association with a district judge. The system proved unsatisfactory both to the judges and to the bar. By the act of February 13, 1801, the number of Supreme Court justices was reduced to five, and their circuit duties were taken away and transferred to newly created circuit judges. There were six circuits with twenty-three districts, and the circuit judges sat independently of the district judges as well as of the supreme bench. The result was a multiplicity of judicial offices and increased annual expenses. The new places had been filled with Federalists by President Adams in the dying hours of his administration, or, to use an expression of Jefferson's, the Federalists retreated into the judiciary as a stronghold.

JUDICIARY DEBATE OF 1802

One of the first acts of Congress after the beginning of Jefferson's administration was the reorganization of the courts and the abolition of these new circuit justiceships. Breckinridge, in the Senate, moved the repealing act, January 8, 1802; and it was carried February 3d, after a spirited debate which turned chiefly upon the constitutionality of the bill. The vote was close, the bill being passed in the Senate by 16 to 15. A prolonged and somewhat acrimonious discussion followed in the House of Representatives. It was exceedingly able, although the historian Henry Adams calls it a dull debate.[1] Many upheld the power of the courts to nullify laws, and even advocates of the repealing bill conceded that this power belonged to the State judiciary. Almost every important consideration presented in the recent debate in Congress upon the Arizona constitution will be found to have been urged in the debate of 1802.

Bayard of Delaware, and Rutledge of South Carolina, were among the leading opponents of the bill in the House. They denied that the State courts had exclusive right to decide upon the validity of laws of Congress. The State tribunals have the right to declare an act of Congress void, said Bayard, but their decisions

[1] *History of U. S.*, i., 286.

are reviewable by the Supreme Court of the Union.　He quoted the twenty-fifth section of the Judiciary Act of 1789, and said:

> Thus as early as the year 1789, among the first acts of the government, the legislature explicitly recognized the right of a state court to declare a treaty, a statute, and authority exercised under the United States, void, subject to the revision of the Supreme Court of the United States; and it has expressly given the final power to the Supreme Court to affirm a judgment which is against the validity either of a treaty, statute, or an authority of the government.[1]

Huger of South Carolina quoted Judge Tucker, Professor of Law in the College of William and Mary, and one of the judges in the Supreme Court of Virginia, who in his treatise upon the State and Federal constitutions had asserted the supremacy of the Federal judiciary and its unquestioned right to override unconstitutional laws.[2]

Tallmadge reminded the House that "when the Constitution was sent to the several States for adoption, every article and clause in it underwent a severe scrutiny and a most critical examination. Perhaps no article was more minutely examined than that which respects the judicial establishment, and from what I then heard and have since been informed, I am induced to believe that the Constitution would not have been adopted, if the independence of your judges had not been deemed to be secured by that instrument."[3]

[1] *Annals of Congress* (7th Cong.), 647, 648.　[2] *Id.*, 679, 680.　[3] *Id.*, 942.

Rutledge,[1] in an elaborate address, reviewed the history of the making of the Constitution. He admitted the argument could not be conclusive because the inquiry was not so much what the Constitution ought to be as what it really is. "If any doubt hangs over its language," said he, "it is fair to ascertain the meaning by recurring to what must have been the wish and the intention of those who framed the instrument." It was, he declared, well known to every member of the House that the right of the State courts to decide upon the constitutionality of State laws had been recognized in the laws themselves, that the power had been exercised by the courts, which had pronounced laws unconstitutional and void, and that not only had these decisions been acquiesced in by the legislature, but that the condemned laws had in fact been removed from the codes of State statutes. Throughout this debate the power of State judges to overthrow unconstitutional laws seems to have been conceded, the contention of the advocates of the bill being that the power did not reside in the Supreme Court of the United States.[2]

The Federalists undeniably went too far in urging that the repeal bill was unconstitutional. There can be no doubt of the power of Congress to abolish an inferior court.[3] As Breckinridge said, "because the

[1] Rutledge is to be distinguished from John Rutledge who was a member of the Federal Convention and afterwards Chief Justice of the Supreme Court of the United States, and from Edward Rutledge who was a member of the South Carolina ratifying convention.

[2] *Annals of Congress* (7th Cong.), 746.

[3] Congress would, I think, be guilty of an unconstitutional act were it to abolish the inferior courts without substituting others in their place if

Constitution provides that the judge shall hold
his office during good behavior, that does not
prevent abolition of his office, where the office
is unnecessary." Breckinridge was among the few
who explicitly denied the power of the courts to
check the legislature. "I would ask," said he,
"where they get the power and who checks the courts
when they violate the Constitution? I deny the
power. If it is derived from the Constitution, I
ask the gentleman to point out the clause which
grants it." Gouverneur Morris, who expressed in
the Federal Convention his conviction that the
judges should have such a power, answering Breckinridge, said:

They derive this authority from a power higher than the
constitution. . . . The judges must declare what the law is.
The decision of the Supreme Court is and of necessity must
be final. Otherwise the moment the legislature declare
themselves supreme, they become so. . . . The sovereignty
of America will no longer reside in the people, but in Congress, and the constitution is whatever they choose to make
it.

---

needed. The Constitution intends that all the judicial power shall actually be vested. This was the view of Marshall, Story, and Webster
and was, I think, accepted until the decision in McCardle's case. Nor
has Congress the power seriously to infringe upon the appellate jurisdiction of the Supreme Court. Although that instrument says that
the appellate jurisdiction is subject to such exceptions as Congress may
make, the power to make exceptions was never intended to permit
Congress to destroy all the appellate jurisdiction of the Court or make
any substantial encroachments upon it. This, too, was the view of
Marshall, Webster, and Story.

DANIEL WEBSTER ON JUDICIAL POWER

To the evidence already marshalled to show that judicial control rests, not upon inference, but upon the express text of the Constitution, and that it was consciously and intentionally bestowed upon the courts by the Convention, there may well be added, because of its importance, the testimony of Daniel Webster. Webster was five years of age when the Convention that framed the Constitution of the United States met at Philadelphia. He grew up in association with men who had fought in the Revolution and devised the present government. He was nearer the English Revolution of 1688 than are we to the Philadelphia Convention of 1787. He knew intimately the work of Hamilton, Madison, Jefferson, Adams, and their contemporaries. He was steeped in the history of the formative days of the Republic. He had seen thirteen colonies expand into thirty states under the influence of a government whose institutions he had profoundly studied. He venerated the Revolutionary patriots and loved the Union with an enthusiasm that was a passion, and next to Marshall upon the bench at Washington did more than any other statesman of the first sixty years of this nation to expound and interpret the Constitution.

Webster's views are lucidly set forth in the Reply to Hayne in the Senate of the United States, January 26 and 27, 1830, in his speech in the Senate February 16, 1833, in reply to Calhoun, in which Webster contended that the Constitution was not a compact between sov-

ereign states, and in his address at a dinner given in his
honor in the City of New York, March 10, 1831.

Hayne, as is well known, had set up the standard of
nullification.   South Carolina repudiated the tariff law
of the United States, and, following in the lead of the
Virginia and Kentucky resolutions, behind which were
the shades of Jefferson and Madison, maintained her
right to treat this legislation as void.   The occasion
called for a crushing answer to this fallacy, and Webster
made it.   He conclusively showed the utter powerless-
ness of a government which lay at the mercy of thirteen
or twenty-four legislatures.   He explained the true
nature of the government created under the Constitution.   It was a government of limited powers.   There
were restrictions upon Congress, and there were also
prohibitions upon the States.   Some authority must
exist with ultimate jurisdiction to fix and ascertain
the interpretation of all grants, restrictions, and prohibitions.

Who [he asked] shall construe this grant of the people?
Who shall interpret their will where it may be supposed
they have left it doubtful?   With whom do they repose this
ultimate right of deciding on the powers of the government?
Sir, they have settled all this in the fullest manner.

.   .   .   .

The Constitution has itself pointed out, ordained, and
established that authority.   How has it accomplished this
great and essential end?   By declaring, Sir, that "*the Constitution, and the laws of the United States made in pursuance thereof, shall be the supreme law of the land, anything*

in the constitution or laws of any State to the contrary not-withstanding."

This, Sir, was the first great step. By this the supremacy of the Constitution and laws of the United States is declared. The people so will it. No State law is to be valid which comes in conflict with the Constitution, or any law of the United States passed in pursuance of it. *But who shall decide this question of interference? To whom lies the last appeal?* This, Sir, the Constitution itself decides also, by declaring, "*that the judicial power shall extend to all cases arising under the Constitution and laws of the United States.*" These two provisions cover the whole ground. They are, in truth, the keystone of the arch! With these it is a government; without them it is a confederation. . . . Here, [he said in conclusion] is a law which is declared to be supreme; and here is a power established which is to interpret that law.

Calhoun, in the Senate, in February, 1833, had argued that the political system established by the Constitution was a compact to which the people of the several States, as separate and sovereign communities, were parties, with the consequence that each of these sovereign parties had the right to judge for itself of any alleged violation of the Constitution by Congress. Webster repelled this idea with all the vigor and eloquence at his command. He elaborated his argument in the Reply to Hayne. He showed that the people, that is the people of all the then existing States, had ordained the Constitution as the fundamental law, that the States, as States, had not entered into a constitution, but that it was the people's Constitution, and that the instrument created direct relations between the new government and individuals. Upon the subject of the judicial power he said:

But, Sir, let us go to the actual formation of the Constitution; let us open the journal of the Convention itself, and we shall see that the very first resolution which the Convention adopted was, "THAT A NATIONAL GOVERNMENT OUGHT TO BE ESTABLISHED, CONSISTING OF A SUPREME LEGISLATURE, JUDICIARY, AND EXECUTIVE."

The object was to supersede the Confederation by a regular government acting directly on individuals. "Allow me," said Webster, "to quote but one or two proofs out of hundreds." Connecticut had sent to the General Convention Samuel Johnson and Oliver Ellsworth. They were also members of the ratifying convention in Connecticut.

On the first day of the debates, being called on to explain the reasons which led the Convention at Philadelphia to recommend such a Constitution, after showing the insufficiency of the existing confederacy, inasmuch as it applied to States, as States, Mr. Johnson proceeded to say:—
" The Convention saw this imperfection in attempting to legislate for States in their political capacity, that the coercion of law can be exercised by nothing but a military force. They have, therefore, gone upon entirely new ground. They have formed one new nation out of the individual States. The Constitution vests in the general legislature a power to make laws in matters of national concern; to appoint judges to decide upon these laws; and to appoint officers to carry them into execution. This

excludes the idea of an armed force.   The power which is
to enforce these laws is to be a legal power, vested in proper
magistrates.   The force which is to be employed is the
energy of law; and this force is to operate only upon individuals who fail in their duty to their country.   This is the
peculiar glory of the Constitution, that it depends upon the
mild and equal energy of the magistracy for the execution
of the laws.

In the further course of the debate, Mr. Ellsworth said :

"In republics, it is a fundamental principle, that the
majority govern, and that the minority comply with the
general voice.   How contrary, then, to republican principles, how humiliating, is our present situation!   A single
State can rise up, and put a *veto* upon the most important
public measures.   We have seen this actually take place;
a single State has controlled the general voice of the Union;
a minority, a very small minority, has governed us.   So far
is this from being consistent with republican principles,
that it is, in effect, the worst species of monarchy.

"Hence we see how necessary for the Union is a coercive
principle.   No man pretends the contrary.   We all see
and feel this necessity.   The only question is, Shall it be
a coercion of law, or a coercion of arms?   There is no other
possible alternative.   Where will those who oppose a coercion of law come out?   Where will they end?   A necessary consequence of their principles is a war of the States one
against another.   I am for coercion by law; that coercion
which acts only upon delinquent individuals.   This Constitution does not attempt to coerce sovereign bodies,
States, in their political capacity.   No coercion is applicable to such bodies, but that of an armed force.   If we
should attempt to execute the laws of the Union by sending
an armed force against a delinquent State, it would involve

the good and bad, the innocent and guilty, in the same
calamity. But this legal coercion singles out the guilty
individual, and punishes him for breaking the laws of the
Union."

Mr. Webster further contended that

it rightfully belongs to Congress and to the courts of the
United States to settle the construction of this supreme
law in doubtful cases. This is denied; and here arises the
great practical question, *Who is to construe finally the Constitution of the United States?* We all agree that the Constitution is the supreme law, but who shall interpret that
law? In our system of the division of powers between different governments, controversies will necessarily sometimes arise respecting the extent of the powers of each.
Who shall decide these controversies? Does it rest with the
general government, in all or any of its departments, to
exercise the office of final interpreter? Or may each of the
States, as well as the general government, claim this right
of ultimate decision?

The Constitution had not "left this cardinal point without full and explicit provision." It was

express and emphatic. It declares that the judicial power
shall extend to all *cases* in law or equity arising under the
Constitution, laws of the United States, and treaties; that
there shall be *one* Supreme Court, and that this Supreme
Court shall have appellate jurisdiction of all these cases,
subject to such exceptions as Congress may make. It is
impossible to escape from the generality of these words. If
a case arises under the Constitution, that is, if a case arises
depending on the construction of the Constitution, the

judicial power of the United States extends to it. It reaches *the case, the question;* it attaches the power of the national judicature to the *case* itself, in whatever court it may arise or exist; and in this *case* the Supreme Court has appellate jurisdiction over all courts whatever. No language could provide with more effect and precision than is here done, for subjecting constitutional questions to the ultimate decision of the Supreme Court. *And, Sir, this is exactly what the Convention found it necessary to provide for, and intended to provide for. It is, too, exactly what the people were universally told was done when they adopted the Constitution.*

There were, said Webster, thirteen judicatures already in existence.

The evil complained of, or the danger to be guarded against, was contradiction and repugnance in the decisions of these judicatures. It was undeniably true that the framers of the Constitution intended to create a national judicial power, which should be paramount on national subjects. And after the Constitution was framed, and while the whole country was engaged in discussing its merits, one of its most distinguished advocates, Mr. Madison, told the people that it *was true, that, in controversies relating to the boundary between the two jurisdictions, the tribunal which is ultimately to decide is to be established under the general government.* Mr. Martin, who had been a member of the Convention, asserted the same thing to the legislature of Maryland, and urged it as a reason for rejecting the Constitution. Mr. Pinckney, himself also a leading member of the Convention, declared it to the people of South Carolina. *Everywhere it was admitted, by friends and foes, that this power was in the Constitution.* By some it was thought dangerous, by most it was thought necessary; but by all it was agreed to be a power actually contained in the instrument. The Convention saw the absolute necessity of some control in the national government over State laws. Different modes of establishing this control were suggested and considered. At one time, it was proposed that the laws of the States should, from time to time, be laid before Congress, and that Congress should possess a negative over them. But this was thought inexpedient and inadmissible; and in its place, and expressly as a substitute for it, the existing provision was introduced; that is to say, a provision by which the federal courts should have authority to over-rule such State laws as might be in manifest contravention of the Constitution. The writers of the *Federalist*, in explaining the Constitution, while it was yet pending before the people, and still unadopted, give this account of the matter in terms, and assign this reason for the article as it now stands. By this provision Congress escaped the necessity of any revision of State laws, left the whole sphere of State legislation quite untouched, and yet obtained a security against any infringement of the constitutional power of the general government. Indeed, Sir, allow me to ask again, if the national judiciary was not to exercise a power of revision on constitutional questions over the judicatures of the States, why was any national judicature erected at all? Can any man give a sensible reason for having a judicial power in this government, unless it be for the sake of maintaining a uniformity of decision on questions arising under the Constitution and laws of Congress, and insuring its execution? And does not this very idea of uniformity necessarily imply that the construction given by the national courts is to be the prevailing construction? How else, Sir, is it possible that uniformity can be preserved?

I think [said Webster] that I cannot do better than

to leave this part of the subject by reading the remarks made upon it in the Convention of Connecticut, by Mr. Ellsworth; a gentleman, Sir, who has left behind him, on the records of the government of his country, proofs of the clearest intelligence and of the deepest sagacity, as well as of the utmost purity and integrity of character. "This Constitution," says he, "defines the extent of the powers of the general government. If the general legislature should, at any time, overleap their limits, the judicial department is a constitutional check. If the United States go beyond their powers, if they make a law which the Constitution does not authorize, it is void; and the judiciary power, the national judges, who, to secure their impartiality, are to be made independent, will declare it to be void. On the other hand, if the States go beyond their limits, if they make a law which is a usurpation upon the general government, the law is void; and upright, independent judges will declare it to be so." Nor did this remain merely matter of private opinion. In the very first session of the first Congress, with all these well-known objects, both of the Convention and the people, full and fresh in his mind, Mr. Ellsworth, as is generally understood, reported the bill for the organization of the judicial department, and in that bill made provision for the exercise of this appellate power of the Supreme Court, in all the proper cases, in whatsoever court arising; and this appellate power has now been exercised for more than forty years, without interruption, and without doubt.

In the speech in New York City, Webster said:

The judicial department, under the Constitution of the United States, possesses still higher duties. . . . The general and State governments, both established by the people,

7

are established for different purposes, and with different powers. Between those powers questions may arise; and who shall decide them? Some provision for this end is absolutely necessary. What shall it be? This was the question before the Convention; and various schemes were suggested. It was foreseen that the States might inadvertently pass laws inconsistent with the Constitution of the United States, or with acts of Congress. At least, laws might be passed which would be charged with such inconsistency. How should these questions be disposed of? Where shall the power of judging, in cases of alleged interference, be lodged?   .   .   .   It was thought wiser and safer, on the whole, to require State legislatures and State judges to take an oath to support the Constitution of the United States, and then leave the States at liberty to pass whatever laws they pleased, and if interference, in point of fact, should arise, to refer the question to judicial decision. To this end, the judicial power, under the Constitution of the United States, was made coextensive with the legislative power. It was extended to all cases arising under the Constitution and the laws of Congress. The judiciary became thus possessed of the authority of deciding, in the last resort, in all cases of alleged interference between State laws and the Constitution and laws of Congress.

There can be no uncertainty what would be Webster's attitude were he alive to-day.

SIMILARITY OF VIEW OF CHIEF JUSTICE GIBSON

There is an interesting coincidence of opinion between Webster and Chief Justice John B. Gibson, of Pennsylvania, commonly regarded as one of the

ablest men who ever sat upon the bench of that
State, a bench renowned for the brilliancy and ability
of its judges. This coincidence has enhanced interest
because, in the judgment of some writers, the opinion
of Judge Gibson in the case of Eakin *v.* Raub, decided
in 1825, contains a formidable argument against the
right of the State judiciary to annul laws of the commonwealth. It has been declared to be a most convincing,
in fact quite unanswerable, argument against the existence as well as against the expediency of the power of
the judiciary to review legislation under any circumstances.[1] Those who appeal to it as a most convincing
argument against judicial control may well be asked
whether that portion of it which deals with the power
of the Federal judiciary must not be accepted as convincing. In contrasting the functions of State and
Federal judges, Chief Justice Gibson said:

But in regard to an act of assembly, which is found to be
in collision with the Constitution, or treaties of the United
States, I take the duty of the judiciary to be exactly the
reverse. By becoming parties to the Federal Constitution,
the States have agreed to several limitations of their individual sovereignty, to enforce which, it was thought to be
absolutely necessary to prevent them from giving effect to
laws in violation of those limitations, through the instrumentality of their own judges. Accordingly, it is declared
in the sixth article and second section of the Federal Constitution, that "This Constitution, and the laws of the
United States which shall be made in pursuance thereof,

[1] "Government by Judiciary," L. B. Boudin, *Political Science Quarterly*, xxvi., 258.

and all treaties made, or which shall be made under the authority of the United States, shall be the supreme law of the land; and the judges in every State shall be bound thereby; anything in the laws or Constitution of any State to the contrary notwithstanding.''

This is an express grant of a political power and it is conclusive to show that no law of inferior obligation, as every State law must necessarily be, can be executed at the expense of the Constitution, laws, or treaties of the United States.

And he concludes:

Unless, then, the respective States are not bound by the engagement, which they have contracted by becoming parties to the Constitution of the United States, they are precluded from denying either the right or the duty of their judges, to declare their laws void when they are repugnant to that Constitution.

The learned Justice was dealing only with the powers of State tribunals. The power of the Supreme Court of the United States is an inevitable corollary, for that Court is expressly made the final authority, and upon writ of error to the State court must either affirm or reverse the decision of the State tribunal, and in doing so must necessarily declare the State law harmonious with or repugnant to the Federal Constitution. So far as Judge Gibson's reasoning extends, it squares completely with Webster's. Webster goes farther and shows the intent of the makers of the Constitution, as construed by their words and by the language of the instrument, to give Federal courts like authority over unconstitutional acts of Congress.

None of Judge Gibson's successors seems to have gone so far as to deny *in toto* the right of the State judiciary to override unconstitutional laws. In one of the leading cases in the State of Pennsylvania,[1] decided in 1853, in which a series of able opinions was delivered, Chief Justice Jeremiah S. Black, whose authority as a constitutional lawyer will be generally conceded, acknowledged that a power resided in the judiciary to annul legislation, but it was a power with limitations. To make the law void "it must be clearly not an exercise of legislative authority, or else be forbidden so plainly, as to leave the case free from all doubt." It was not the principle, but an unwarrantable extension of it against which Judge Black revolted. The Court had been asked, as he said, to hold a law, though not prohibited, "void if it violates the spirit of our institutions, or impairs any of those rights which it is the object of a free government to protect, and to declare it unconstitutional if it be wrong and unjust. But we cannot do this." The rule that should govern the judiciary forbade it to declare an act of assembly void save where "it violates the constitution clearly, palpably, plainly, and in such manner as to leave no doubt or hesitation in our minds." These words recognize the power of the Court, while they restrict it within its appropriate boundaries. Such a decision cannot be cited as proof that the courts possess no power whatever over unconstitutional legislation.

It will, I think, be found that in most if not all the later decisions, both State and Federal, questioning

[1] Sharpless *v.* The Mayor, 21 Penn. State, 147.

the extent of judicial power, the controversy was not whether the courts could set aside a law plainly and palpably unconstitutional, but whether they could do so because they deemed the law opposed to the spirit pervading the Constitution, or to the fundamental rights of property or to principles of justice. Such a power, as Mr. Justice Clifford of the United States Supreme Court well said, "is denied to the courts, because to concede it would be to make the courts sovereign over both the Constitution and the people, and convert the government into a judicial despotism."

No one has stated the true boundaries of the power in better phrase than did Iredell while sitting as Justice of the Supreme Court of the United States, in the case of Calder v. Bull, decided in 1798.[1] Although loyal to his earlier convictions as to the right of the judiciary to set aside laws in conflict with the Constitution, he nevertheless refused assent to the doctrine that "a legislative act against natural justice must in itself be void." An act of Congress or of the legislature of a State that distinctly violates constitutional provisions is, said he, unquestionably void. The frontier line of clear power was thus marked by him:

As the authority to declare it [a legislative act] void is of a delicate and awful nature, the Court will never resort to that authority, but in a clear and urgent case. If, on the other hand, the legislature of the Union, or the legislature of any member of the Union, shall pass a law, within the general scope of their constitutional power, the court cannot

[1] 3 Dallas, 386.

pronounce it to be void, merely because it is, in their judgment, contrary to the principles of natural justice.

The argument that has been combated is, not that the
courts may never have abused a power plainly reposed
in them, but that the courts possess no power at all to
set a law aside.   The specific fallacy sought to be ex-
posed is that the Convention that framed the Constitution did not mean to repose in the judiciary any
power to condemn unconstitutional legislation and that
the courts of the States which ratified the Constitution
never possessed any such authority.

Again and again has it been asserted by the cham-
pions of judicial recall that the precedents in the early
States were few and unimportant, that persons in other
States were not aware of the decisions in a particular
State, that there was little if any interchange of opinion,
that there were no newspapers of consequence when
the Convention of 1787 sat, and that there was no
general acceptance of the doctrine of judicial control.

If these modern sciolists are to be credited, few
persons gave any heed to the burning eloquence of
James Otis, or to Justice William Cushing's charge to
the Massachusetts jury or to John Adams's public
approval of it; few were aware of the decision in the
Mayor's Court of New York City upon the famous
trespass act, of the storm of protest which it aroused,
or the resolution of the Assembly which it evoked; or
knew of the cogent argument of Varnum in Trevett v.
Weeden, of the unanimous opinion of the judges in that
celebrated case, or the futile attempt of the legislature

of Rhode Island to discipline them; or the controversy
which aroused the State of North Carolina in Bayard *v.*
Singleton.   Few persons, we are asked to assume, knew
of Iredell's "Letter of an Elector" in the summer of
1786, his reply to Spaight in August, 1787, or his published answer to George Mason's "Objections to the
Constitution"[1]; few persons ever read Hamilton's convincing defence of the judicial power in the *Federalist*
or his splendid appeals to the New York ratifying
convention, or heard of Ellsworth's or Johnson's
arguments for the new judiciary in the Connecticut
ratifying convention; or, although in the Virginia
Convention (as in others) the Constitution was discussed
clause by clause, heard of Patrick Henry's lengthy and
eloquent denunciation of it,—although Henry was,
perhaps, the greatest orator of his day,—or knew of the
replies of Madison, or Marshall, in that body; or of
Wilson's speeches in the Pennsylvania Convention, or
Charles Pinckney's arguments in the South Carolina
Convention, or Davie's and Iredell's in the first North
Carolina Convention, or read the debates in the first
session of Congress when the judiciary act of 1789 was
framed.

What we wish, says Dean Trickett, "is authentic
evidence that a majority of the ratifying majorities of
the ratifying conventions, at the moment of ratification,

[1] Richard Henry Lee, one of Virginia's most formidable opponents
of the new Constitution, "appealed to the world through the press in a
series of 'Letters from the Federal Farmer' of which thousands of copies
were scattered through the central states." Lee disseminated in Philadelphia not only his own objections but also George Mason's "Objections to the Constitution" (Bancroft, vi., 374, 383).

understood that they were conferring and intended to
confer on the courts a power to annul statutes of Congress." Evidence of such far-reaching nature is mani-
festly impossible. As well ask proof that the vote by
which the Fourteenth Amendment to the Federal Constitution was ratified was with conscious knowledge of
the scope of that amendment or that any great principle
which has been submitted to referendum was understood
in a specific manner by a majority of its approvers. In
these pages has, however, been massed evidence such
as would determine the action of prudent men in matters of importance, that the assertion of the right of the
judiciary to control legislation was well known. Never
in the history of the nation was discussion of public
questions relatively more general or intelligent. The
argument of our modern teachers requires the assumption that Webster's studies of the origin of the Constitution were built upon fallacies, that his Reply to Hayne,
which at one bound gave him a great national reputation
and led to the dinner in New York at which Chancellor Kent presided, contained false, unhistorical statements, and that his defence of the judicial power, long
treated by scholars and thinkers as conclusive, was
utterly unsound and not the brilliant and unanswerable
argument which the country at large deemed it to be.
Furthermore, the argument of these teachers ignores
altogether the inevitable conclusion to be drawn from
the substitution of the Martin resolution of July 17,
1787, for Madison's plan of a Council of Revision and
the process of evolution step by step into the supreme
law clause of the Constitution, which, with its "twin

text" (section 2, Article III.), became, in the language of Charles Pinckney and Webster, the keystone of the arch upon which the government was founded.

Enough has been quoted from debates and letters to refute the unfounded charge, so often heard to-day, that the Convention met in secrecy to frame a government that was undemocratic. Secrecy was deemed essential in the drafting of the Constitution in order to insure definite action. The widest publicity was immediately afterwards given to the Convention's work. No part received more thorough explanation or was the subject of fuller discussion than its plan for the judicial department. In no spirit of dislike to democracy, but with the broadest vision, the framers of the Constitution resolved upon

AN INDEPENDENT JUDICIARY

How to secure judicial independence was a profoundly important question. The Convention had before it experience both in England and in the original States of the Union. There was the light of experience in England, which upon the accession of William of Orange had vested in Parliament all power of removal of judges. That the full jurisdiction of Parliament might not be impaired by a royal pardon, the same act that took away from the king his old power to unseat judges provided that no pardon under the great seal of England should ever be pleadable to an impeachment by the House of Commons. This meant that the king by a pardon should not be able to shield an unrighteous judge from deposition by the legislature.   There was also the light of experience in the several States.[1] All the thirteen States had erected their judicial systems upon this model, providing fixity of tenure during good behavior and the process of impeachment for judicial wrongdoing.

To emancipate judges from all temptation to subserviency to the legislature the new Constitution provided that their salaries should not be subject to diminution. Thus the independence of the judge was safeguarded. With the same end in view, appointment was kept from control by the legislative department,—the department whose work it would become the duty of the courts to interpret and review.

As was said by Hamilton in the *Federalist*,[2] the

[1] The power of the crown to terminate the official life of a judge ceased with the Revolution of 1688.   The constitutional guarantee erected by Parliament against further subversion of judicial independence, which took the form of a withdrawal to itself of all power of removal, has been curiously misconstrued in this country. The English statute lies at the basis of the constitutions of several of the eastern States— New Hampshire, Massachusetts, Connecticut, Rhode Island.   It has been erroneously assumed that the English statute gave the right of removal arbitrarily and without reason.   The language seems to import such broad authority, although no such power has ever been exercised by Parliament.   The intention of Parliament was not to remove without cause.   It was to take away from the *king* all power of this sort and not to leave in him any vestige of authority.   Had the act of Parliament given that body power to remove for cause, the implication might have been that power of removal without cause remained with the sovereign. In most of the States of the Union the legislature removes only for good cause.

[2] LXXVIII.

Convention "acted wisely in copying from the models of those constitutions which have established good behavior as the tenure of judicial offices in point of duration." The plan, he added, "would have been inexcusably defective, if it had wanted this important feature of good government. The experience of Great Britain affords an illustrious comment on the excellence of the institution." Elsewhere in the same paper he declared that

the standard of good behavior for the continuance in office of the judicial magistracy, is certainly one of the most valuable of the modern improvements in the practice of government. In a monarchy it is an excellent barrier to the despotism of the prince: in a republic, it is a no less excellent barrier to the encroachments and oppressions of the representative body. And it is the best expedient which can be devised in any government to secure a steady, upright, and impartial administration of the laws. . . .

Nothing can contribute so much to its [the judiciary's] firmness and independence as permanency in office. This quality may therefore be justly regarded as an indispensable ingredient in its constitution; and in a great measure as the CITADEL of the public justice and the public security.

Similar ideas may be found in utterances of other influential members of the Federal Convention and of delegates to the ratifying conventions.[1] They were

[1] In his earlier years Jefferson himself entertained like views. In a letter to George Wythe with whom he studied law, whom he declares

too close in time to the days when the king had tyrannized over the English judges not to appreciate the necessity of judicial independence. Page after page might be quoted from speeches in the ratifying conventions to show that the sentiment which the Federal Convention reflected in its plan of an independent judiciary pervaded the entire country. Upon this substantial basis was the judicial fabric reared. With adamantine firmness has it thus far withstood every assault upon it. Under the dominance of the notion prevailing in the middle of the last century that popular elections were a solvent for all political ills, the judiciary in many States was made elective, but the swing of the

---

to have been his "mentor," and with whom he maintained an unbroken friendship for forty years, he wrote in July, 1776, as follows:

"The dignity and stability of government in all its branches, the morals of the people, and every blessing of society, depend so much upon an upright and skilful administration of justice, that the judicial power ought to be distinct from both the legislature and executive, and independent upon both that so it may be a check upon both, as both should be checks upon that. The judges, therefore, should always be men of learning and experience in the laws, of exemplary morals, great patience, calmness, and attention; their minds should not be distracted with jarring interests; they should not be dependent upon any man or body of men. To these ends they should hold estates for life in their offices, or, in other words, their commissions should be during good behavior, and their salaries ascertained and established by law."

He wrote to Archibald Stuart on December 23, 1791:

"Render the judiciary respectable by every possible means, to wit, firm tenure in office, competent salaries, and reduction of their numbers. Men of high learning and abilities are few in every country; and by taking in those who are not so, the able part of the body have their hands tied by the unable. This branch of the government will have the weight of the conflict on their hands, because they will be the last appeal of reason."

pendulum has been from short to longer terms, in other words, backwards in the direction of life tenure. Human invention never devised a better method than the appointive system with tenure during good behavior.

ELECTION OF FEDERAL JUDGES NO REMEDY

To adopt the elective method in the case of Federal judges would be a dangerous departure from a system that has worked admirably for more than a hundred years. The proponents of such a method have never gone so far as to determine whether they would favor a national election law, thus centralizing power in the general government, or a law which would give the States, as States, a voice in the election of the judiciary, thus bringing Federal courts under State control. The appointment of judges by a president or governor is far preferable to their selection by machine leaders, which is what the present convention system means. No traffic is too despicable, no bargain too nefarious, for a boss; no interest, however sinister, hesitates to approach him. Choice of judges by direct nominations is out of the question. The eulogists of an omnipotent Parliament should remember that England appoints her judiciary.

It cannot be shown that under the appointive system judges have been more susceptible to corrupt influences than under an elective one. In the address from which I have quoted Judge Clark admits that the judges of the United States Supreme Court have never been charged with being corruptly influenced. That, unfortunately, has not been true of an elective judiciary, for it has not only been charged, but proved, that elective judges have in some instances been corrupt. Nor do "big business" or "corporate interests" have more sway with appointed, than with elected, judges, nor can it be proved that the appointive system lends itself more to conservative influences. Probably the Supreme Court of the United States is to-day more responsive to the popular desire for melioristic legislation than are the highest tribunals in some States where judges are elected.

The chief purpose of an elective system is to establish some degree of control over judges, so that they may not become arbitrary and lose all sense of responsibility to the people. Jefferson's great fear was that judges who were not elected, and were not readily removable, would become autocratic. On the other hand, the theory of the creators of the present judicial system was that a judge should be placed beyond the menace of recall, except for failure in performance of duty. Impeachment can be made a live remedy, as can also removability for cause. The demand for recall springs, however, not so much from doubt of the integrity of the courts as from dislike of their decisions. To enforce recall because decisions are repugnant to the popular wish is to make judges dependent on popular will alone for the tenure of their offices, and this is to take a fatal step backwards, and in the name of progress.[1]

[1] Arbitrary recall of judges by the legislature is not only wrong in principle but would prove impracticable. It is said that the legislature

JUDICIAL RECALL A FALLACY

Such fallacies as judicial recall originate in the gravest and most fundamental misconceptions of the social state. We hear much about the rule of the people, and the rights of the people,—phrases that are too often catchwords unless the limitations which they require be kept in mind. It may shock the unreflecting to hear that the rule of the people would be synonymous with anarchy—but this is strictly true.

of New York may remove judges without assigning reason, although this construction of the constitution seems to me doubtful. Suppose that the alleged power had been invoked against the Court of Appeals judges in the Ives case—the result merely would have been to convert the legislature into an arena in which the reasons for and against the Court's decision would have been presented. Cogent reasons could have been advanced to support the Court's view, and against it. Suppose the panacea, now urged by Senator Owen, of having the Federal judges removed by Congress without cause had been in effect when the income tax cases were decided? A motion in Congress to remove the Supreme Court justices would simply have transferred to Congress discussion of the reasons for and against the constitutionality of the law. Only in times of intense popular excitement such as prevailed during the Johnson impeachment proceedings in 1868, would there be a chance of removing the judges. The strain upon the institutions of the country would be one which it could not long endure.

Were Congress actually to remove the judges, could its decision be said to accord with the *popular will*? Properly the power of removal could be exercised only by a Congress elected upon that issue, and what friend of his country would wish to see such an issue injected into politics? A Congress not elected for that purpose would be acting arbitrarily in the removal; and if members who voted for it should lose their seats, would that be evidence that the removal was not in accordance with popular will? A vote to remove would at best represent the wish of a temporary majority, and government by a temporary majority would soon usher in anarchy. To have a popular vote for removal, or recall by the people, is unthinkable.

The rule of the people so called is, and in the nature of things must be, the rule of a temporary majority. When all legislation is on a par with the organic law the Constitution will be atrophied and will disappear. The legislature will become supreme, the judiciary sink to inferior place. Is it by enthronement of the popular will that Utopia is to be found? In the debates upon the Arizona constitution it was often urged that the people could be trusted. By the people, is meant the majority, and the majority is never static, but always mobile. Both Plato and Aristotle agreed in denouncing government in which the opinion of a majority had unrestrained sway. In extreme democracy, according to Aristotle,

the law was disregarded that the people might rule; the magistrates were dethroned. The people were told that they were the best judges, they gladly received the invitation to judge. . . . There is no constitution, where there is no law. There is nothing fixed or determined; life is a chaos in which anything may happen, but nothing can be foreseen.

Burke, one of the greatest of political philosophers, and one of the sincerest friends of the people, who believed that "in all disputes between the people and their rulers, the presumption is at least upon a par in favor of the people," never wearied in insisting that law and arbitrary power of any kind were in eternal enmity.

Judges are guided and governed by the eternal laws of justice, to which we are all subject. We may bite our

8

chains if we will, but we shall be made to know ourselves
and be taught that man is born to be governed by law; and
he that will substitute *will* in the place of it is an enemy to
God. . . .

Against that worst of evils, the government of will and
force instead of wisdom and justice, fixed rules must be
established. The passions not only of individuals, but of
the mass and body of men must be brought into subjection
and their *will* controlled. This can only be done by a power
out of themselves, and not in the exercise of its functions
subject to that will and to those passions which it is its
office to bridle and subdue. *In this sense, the restraints on
men, as well as their liberties, are to be reckoned among their
rights.*

The same idea was splendidly stated by Mr. Evarts
in the New York State constitutional convention of
1867 when he declared the judiciary

the representative of the *justice* of the state, not its
power. . . . The judge is not to declare the will of the
sovereignty, whether that sovereignty reside in a crowned
king, or an aristocracy, or in the unnumbered and unnamed
mass of the people. . . . Justice is of universal import, of
universal necessity, under whatever form of society.

Every society that fails to do justice stands, as Burke
declared, self-condemned; and, as Evarts said, it is the
law of the land that the judges are to declare, and "not
the *will* of any power in the land." The absolute will
of a majority is no more likely to accord with fundamental principles of justice than the absolute will of a
tyrant.

These are not sentiments for a particular epoch, but for all time. To assume that society can ever be constructed upon any other principles is like assuming that we may get beyond the influence of the law of gravitation.

REFORM THROUGH CONSTITUTIONAL METHODS

The Constitution is not an enemy to progress. In every enlightened State it is, or can be made, its instrument. Every State constitution is alterable or can readily be altered at the will of the people. However rigid the national Constitution may seem, it can be changed whenever the people will. The despots (as some think them) who framed and adopted it did not forge chains that could be broken only by a revolution; they provided two simple methods by which change, however far-reaching, could be made whenever the people so willed. This is the only proper remedy for judicial decisions according with law, if the people are dissatisfied with the law.

That remedy is invokable. It involves no cataclysms, no revolutions. If the people of the United States should come to believe their judiciary despotic and obstructive of laws wisely framed for the public welfare, the judges may easily be taught to know their proper limitations. Let it be understood that no law shall be set aside as unconstitutional unless, as the older judges uniformly expressed the idea, it is plainly and palpably so. The application of this formula should be easy.

No law responds to this test when the court is seriously divided regarding it. A statute which three judges out of seven or four out of nine deem constitutional is not "plainly and palpably unconstitutional," and no bench by any vain show of reasoning however elaborate can make it appear to be so.

Furthermore, if by a unanimous or nearly unanimous vote judges declare a statute to be in conflict with the organic law, give the State through its Attorney-General the right of a rehearing. Let the people thus be heard before the court, if need be.

Lastly, so amend the Federal judiciary act or the Constitution of the United States that every case in which due process of law is invoked against a statute designed to ameliorate human conditions may by appeal or upon writ of error be carried to the highest court of the nation. The language of the 14th Amendment that no State shall "deprive any person of life, liberty, or property without due process of law" is, in effect, the language of every State constitution. Forty-eight interpretations of these words should not be possible. Had the judiciary act permitted, the Ives case, which, according to the New York Court of Appeals, offended against this clause of the State and the national Constitution, would have been reviewed in the Supreme Court. With one final tribunal to determine whether any statute, State or Federal, conflicts with the due process clause, there will be evolved a clear definition of the clause; there will also be harmony in decisions. Furthermore, attention will be focalized upon the court that possesses this final authority in every case involving this provision.

To combat and, if possible, refute a widespread error which almost portends a sectional division between east and west has been my purpose. I have endeavored to show that the power of declaring laws unconstitutional laws was exercised by the State judges when the Union was formed; that it was recognized as proper in the resolution which the Congress of the Confederation sent with its letter to the States in April, 1787; that it was expressly granted to the Federal judges by the national Constitution; and is not a usurpation or a novelty. Ours is and has always been a government of *laws*, not of men. A government of laws presupposes a fundamental law, written or unwritten, with which all legislation should harmonize, and the existence of an authority to determine whether a law conflicts with the Constitution. Through all our history the power has rested with the judiciary. A government of men makes the human will supreme. That I contend has never been our system. The people, in whom all power ultimately rests, may change the government; but let the philosophy of all ages and the truth of history be heard before we decide to commit all our ventures—our lives, liberty, and property—to the frail bark steered by a popular majority under the captaincy of the popular will. Such a course is both unwise and unnecessary for people living under constitutional forms of government which may be changed by constitutional methods whenever and as often as a majority may desire.

INDEX

A

Adams, Henry, *History of the United States* by, 2, 85
Adams, John, 19, 84, 89, 103
"American Doctrine of Judicial Power" (by William M. Meigs), 9
American Law Review, citations from, 9, 20
Appointive judges, remarks on, 110, 111
Aragonese, the, Judiciary of, Dr. Robertson, on, 20; Dickinson on, 60
Aristotle, 113
Arizona Constitution, 85, 113
Assembly of New York, Protest of, against Decision in Rutgers *v.* Waddington, 27

B

Baldwin, Abraham (Ga.), 82
Bancroft, George, *History of the United States*, 7, 19, 28, 72, 104
Bassett, Richard (Delaware), 82
Bayard, James A. (Delaware), 85
Bayard *v.* Singleton, 31, 32, 44, 70, 104
Beard, Charles A., of Columbia University, 57
Becket, à, Thomas, 13
Benson, Egbert, 24
Black, Jeremiah S. (Pennsylvania), 101
Blackstone, Sir William, 9, 14, 27
Blair, John, Chancellor (Virginia), 22, 57, 58, 68
Bluntschli, 10, 12
Breckinridge, John, 85, 87, 88
Burke, Edmund, 113, 114

C

Calder *v.* Bull, 102
Calhoun, John C., 89, 91
Canon law, 10, 13

Index

Virginia, Ratifying Convention in, 65
Virginia Resolutions, 83

W

Washington, George (Va.), 76
Webster, Daniel, 39, 56, 88, 89, 90, 94, 96, 97, 98, 100, 105, 106
William of Orange, 106
Wilson, James, 53, 55, 58, 60, 61, 63, 64, 65, 104
Wythe, George, 22, 68, 82, 108

www.ingramcontent.com/pod-product-compliance
Lightning Source LLC
Chambersburg PA
CBHW031945190326
41519CB00007B/665